GHOST STORIES OF NOVA SCOTIA

VERNON OICKLE

MacIntyre Purcell Publishing Inc.
194 Hospital Rd.
Lunenburg, Nova Scotia
B0J 2C0
(902) 640-3350

www.macintyrepurcell.com
info@macintyrepurcell.com

Printed and bound in Canada by Marquis.

Design and layout: Channel Communications and Alex Hickey

Library and Archives Canada Cataloguing in Publication
Oickle, Vernon, 1961-, author   Ghost stories of Nova Scotia /
Vernon Oickle.

Issued in print and electronic formats.ISBN 978-1-927097-77-9 (paperback).--ISBN 978-1-927097-78-6 (pdf).--ISBN 978-1-927097-79-3 (kindle).--ISBN 978-1-927097-80-9 (epub)

    1. Ghosts--Nova Scotia. I. Title.

GR113.5.N69O42 2015   398.209716'05
C2015-904083-3   C2015-904084-1

MacIntyre Purcell Publishing Inc. would like to acknowledge the financial support of the Government of Canada through Department of Canadian Heritage (Canada Book Fund) and the Nova Scotia Department of Tourism, Culture and Heritage.

Dedicated to my good friends,
the members of the Crossed Over Paranormal Group:
Linda Rafuse
Linda Moulton
Kelly Connolly
Evan Rafuse
Lindsay Ingram
Stevie Hatt
Brittany Wolfe
Irene Hupman
Donna Doucette

Foreword

So you picked up this book because you would like to read about ghost stories of Nova Scotia. Well, I can't think of a better author and journalist to bring you through a ghost story as though you were there, but my good friend of many years, Vernon Oickle.

Vernon and I grew up in Liverpool, a little town along the South Shore where almost every household had stories to tell of superstition and ghosts. We share this great friendship because of our love for history and the paranormal.

Living my teen years in a house that had plenty of paranormal activity, it's always great to have friends, like Vernon, who share your love in telling and listening to your experiences. It was our good fortune that upon graduating from school, Vernon decided to choose a career in journalism. In 1982, he completed those studies in Lethbridge, Alberta, returning home to begin a career in the newspaper world. He has gone on to win many regional, national and international awards for his writing and photography, for which his friends and family are very proud. He never forgot his love for ghost stories and superstition, and could now tell these stories to the world with the skill and passion needed. With that, Vernon started publishing his books on the paranormal.

In my job, as manager of a county museum, I work in a building that contains a good amount of paranormal activity. What museum doesn't? Because of that, it was here that a paranormal team of investigators was born. Vernon has been a great supporter and honourary member of our group as we travel Southwest Nova Scotia investigating homes and businesses as requested. In some of those investigations, and with recommendations from Vernon, we have been fortunate to validate a number of the great stories that he shares in his books.

As a writer of great maritime ghost stories, Vernon's books will see readers, generations from now, carrying forward the ghost stories of our day. So, yes, you've picked the right book. Enjoy reading all about ghosts of Nova Scotia.

—*Linda Rafuse, Director Queens County Museum,*
and Lead Investigator Crossed Over Paranormal Society
Liverpool, Nova Scotia

From the Author

Are you afraid of things that go bump in the night? Have you ever thought you saw something from the corner of your eye only to discover there was nothing there?

Have you ever had the feeling that someone was watching you but you are certain that you are alone? Does the sound of your house creaking remind you of footsteps as if someone is coming up the stairs or down the hallway, only there is no one in the house but you? Have you ever had the sensation that someone has touched you or that someone has just rushed past you, only you didn't see anything? Have the doors or windows in your house ever opened and closed on their own? Has something you own ever gone missing only to turn up in the most unusual of places?

If you've answered yes to even one of these questions, then it's just possible that you have encountered a ghost, specter, spirit, apparition or poltergeist. Call it whatever you want, but chances are great that in Nova Scotia, if you have experienced any of these sensations, then there may be another worldly explanation for what happened to you, as ghosts are known to roam throughout the province. I've seen them, felt them, experienced them and best of all, I have met many others who have had similar experiences.

Over the years, I have had the distinct pleasure of meeting many individuals who have welcomed me into their homes or invited me into their places of business to talk about their paranormal experiences. When it comes to ghostly encounters, everyone's experience is different. Some people embrace and welcome the spirit, while others are reluctant believers, readily admitting that they have always been sceptical until their minds were suddenly changed by the unexpected or the inexplicable. But that's okay, because everyone reacts differently to things that can't be easily rationalized. The important thing, however, is to keep an open mind and never judge another person's experiences.

I never tell anyone I don't believe what they've told me simply because there is no way I could possibly know for certain what they've seen, heard or experienced. The paranormal world is very unpredictable, as the spirits exist on a different plane, and those who encounter a ghost or spirit are often caught off guard and are left unsure of what they experienced. For that reason, it is sometimes easy to dismiss or ridicule the witness as they relay their stories, but as a researcher and writer of ghost stories, I invite you to suspend your disbelief and to simply enjoy these tales of the paranormal. Set aside your scepticism and suspend your logic because such rationale has no place in this world.

Within the pages of this book, you are going to meet people who have willingly shared their stories with me. While admitting that they accept, there are people who don't believe or understand what they have experienced. They stand behind what they've told me because to them, their ghostly encounters are very real. Occasionally, however, we meet people who are so intimidated by fears of ridicule from others that they have only agreed to share their stories on the condition of anonymity.

While I have limited the number of anonymous sources in this collection, I have included a few because, honestly, their compelling stories are so provocative and unusual that they deserve to be told. On behalf of these individuals, I encourage you to read their stories and, even if something sounds extreme, be prepared to dismiss your disbelief.

Thank you to everyone who shared his or her story with me. This book would not be possible without you and you have my deepest respect and appreciation. Thank you as well to my friend and publisher John MacIntyre who continues to have faith in me. This book would not be possible were it not for him and the other talented people at MacIntyre Purcell Publishing Inc. Thank you to my family, and especially my wonderful wife, Nancy, who is not only my travelling companion, but also my navigator. She has saved the day more than once. And finally, thank you to all those people who continued to support me throughout the years as I've taken this unusual journey into the world of the paranormal.

Now, read on … if you dare!

— *Vernon Oickle*

Contents

Foreword 4

From the Author 6

On the Cover 11

When the Bell Tolls 15

There's a Ghost in the House 21

The Hand 27

The Lady on the Lake 33

Ghosts at the Cooper's Inn 37

The Hand on the Rock 43

Ghosts in the Bay 49

'Inn' the spirit 51

Haunted Halifax 59

The Man Upstairs 69

The Face in the Mirror 73

Gone With the Wind 79

The Loyalist Ghosts 85

The Haunting of Seminary House 93

This Ghost Horses Around 97

Ghosts at the Galley 103

The Ghosts of Louisbourg 109

The Lady in Blue 113

Whatever Became of Ivy? 119

The Bilingual Ghost 127

The Vampire of Ingonish 135

The Blue Nun of St. Francis Xavier University 139

Ghost Ships 145

Island Lore 151

Local Legends: Sasquatch, Werewolves and UFOs . . . 157

On the Cover

Legend suggests that the historical Academy school in Lunenburg
is haunted.

As we've already established, when it comes to ghost stories, there are plenty of skeptics, but some ghost stories in Nova Scotia have been around so long that they have become engrained in their communities, having evolved into local legends and folklore. One such story surrounds the historical Academy school in the town of Lunenburg.

Built in 1894 –1895, the Lunenburg Academy is a rare, surviving example of Nova Scotia's 19th Century Academy system of secondary education and represents the short and final "golden age" of Academy construction in the province. Its combination of scale, design and function, and the intricacy of detail in its wooden construction, make it unique among comparable educational buildings in Canada.

This remarkable building, an architectural masterpiece, is a landmark in Lunenburg. The unusual architectural style, enhanced by an abundance of decorative Victorian designs, sometimes referred to by the term "Gingerbread," creates a unique structure and it is also allegedly haunted.

The Academy, owned by the Town of Lunenburg, housed Grades 1 through 12 until 1965, when a new high school was built. It continued as an elementary school (Primary to Grade 5) until 2011, when the new Bluenose Academy opened its doors. Today, it is being converted into a multi-purpose cultural institution.

Through the efforts of the Lunenburg Academy Foundation, the Lunenburg Academy, on March 20, 1984, received the official designation of a provincial heritage property. Also, on March 6, 1984, the Historic Sites and Monuments Board of Canada approved the Academy as a site of both national and architectural significance.

It's over a century old, overlooks the town of Lunenburg from Gallows Hill and is surrounded on three sides by a cemetery. Little wonder that generations of Lunenburgers believe that the historic Lunenburg Academy has ghosts.

When the Academy was built, there were two sites chosen as possibilities to place the building — over on Blockhouse Hill or on Gallows Hill. It was a very controversial issue at the time because the latter site, which, as its name suggests, was the scene of at least three hangings.

Along with the execution of two convicted murderers, siblings known as the Boutilier brothers, perhaps the best-remembered hanging in Lunenburg was that of Peter Mailman, which took place in the decade preceding construction of the new school.

Legend goes that he and his wife, Mary, went berry picking. She took a basket and he, an axe. Apparently, Mary didn't come back. When Peter was executed on Gallows Hill, it is said that 2,000 people came out to watch him hang. Because he was a convicted criminal, the body of Peter Mailman was not interred in the Christian cemetery but was buried instead in the backyard of the jailhouse.

The hangings did not stop public officials from deciding to build the new school on the site of the criminals' demise. During the years that followed, reports of strange happenings, usually occurring in the bowels of the three-storey structure, became commonplace. Generations of Lunenburgers, many of them fraught with superstitions garnered during their seafaring days, believe that the historic Lunenburg Academy is home to more than just mere mortals.

One of the more popular "stories" involving the Academy has it that when small children went to the washroom in the basement, they always went with a friend because every now and then, a hand was said to come up out of the toilet and grab the kids.

While no one was ever actually grabbed by this ghostly hand, for some young minds such as those of the primary school students, going through those big, dark corridors would conjure up images. Most children would not go to the basement alone. Instead, they went in twos.

So, is the century-old school really haunted? Only the ghosts know for sure.

When the Bell Tolls

When Carrie moved into the apartment located on the second floor of a stately and historic home in the town of Yarmouth, she admits to being a little apprehensive about the location because of the ghost stories she had heard surrounding the place.

"So here I was," she begins. "A young, single woman, living alone and moving into an apartment that I heard was haunted." She chuckles nervously and adds, "You have to ask, was I crazy? Well, maybe I was, but I really liked the apartment and it was within my budget."

"It was nice and clean and the owners had just done some extensive renovations to the place, so it was in good shape and it was in my price range," she explains. "So, despite all the stories I had heard about the place being haunted, and despite my mother begging me not to take the place because she was really freaked out over the ghosts that live there, I went for it. I thought most of what I had heard was probably nothing more than stories, so to me, it was worth the risk."

However, within days after she had moved in, Carrie began to wonder if maybe she had made a bad decision.

"At first, I thought that maybe it was just my imagination taking over," she says. "You know how the mind will play tricks on you, and once someone plants a seed like that, you have to wonder if what you're experiencing is real or are you just imagining it? That's kind of where I was at that point — was this really happening or was my mind playing tricks on me? But after only a few days of living in the place, I really began to wonder if I was losing my mind."

She first noticed the strange phenomena on the third day after she moved in. It was in early May and the weather was nice, she recalls, so she had several of the apartment windows open to allow the fresh air to get inside.

"The owners had just finished painting only a few days before I moved in, so I could still smell the paint fumes," she says. "I thought I'd take advantage of the nice spring weather we were having to air the place out some. However, about an hour later, I was forced to close the windows because I could hear the sounds of bells ringing and it was so loud that I couldn't hear my music. I had no idea where the bells were coming from, but I assumed the sound was coming from outside."

She assumed wrong.

"Actually," she says, "even after I closed the windows, the noise became louder than ever. It was the strangest thing. I even went downstairs and outside so I could try to figure out where the bells were coming from."

However, Carrie points out, much to her dismay, after she got outside, she could no longer hear the bells.

"That's when I really started freaking out," she admits. "Honestly, how could that be?"

That was the question Carrie had asked herself many times over the 14 months she lived in the apartment.

"But I couldn't handle it anymore so I finally had to move out," she says. Besides the ringing bells, she explains, "it was also the other unexplained things going

16

on in the apartment that finally forced her to move out. The ringing was one thing and that was bad enough," she says.

"But when other strange things started happening in that apartment, I knew it was time to get the heck out of there. At first, the phenomena were subtle. You know, it was things like doors opening and closing on their own, especially in the bedroom and kitchen, and things going missing," she says. "But when I started seeing what I thought were images of a man throughout the apartment, then I started to freak out just a little bit, because the first thing I thought about was that maybe, all those stories I had heard when I was growing up might actually be true."

While the spirit continued to haunt her, Carrie says the incident that really scared her was the night she awoke and saw someone — she's pretty sure it was a man — standing at the foot of the bed and looking down at her.

"I couldn't see his face," she remembers. "It was late and really dark in the room and he was wearing a big hat and an overcoat of some kind with a high collar up over most of his face, so I couldn't really get a good look at him. I just screamed and pulled the covers over my head. I didn't know what else to do, but I can tell you that I was terrified."

She's not really sure how long she lay there under the covers, but she's sure it was several minutes and when she finally found the courage to push the covers down, she was relieved to discover the man in black was gone.

"I have no idea who he was, where he came from, where he went or what he wanted," Carrie says, "but I can tell you he scared the bejesus out of me and it was right around that time that I finally decided I had to move out of this place. I really didn't want to leave because I did it like it there — except for the ghost of course. But I just didn't feel comfortable after that. I just couldn't relax."

She blames her own self for getting into a situation where she had to move out just a year after she moved in.

"It was a real pain," she says. "Because it meant I had to rent a moving truck and I had to find people to help me move, but because of the ringing bells, the man in black and all the other things going on in that apartment, I really felt I had no choice. I just couldn't stay there. I will say though, that my mother was very relieved when I moved out. I can only imagine how she would have felt if I had told her everything that had happened in that place. I'm sure she would have had my dad come over and carry me out. That's how much she believed in those stories."

One final incident, just days before she gave her notice to the landlord, left her with little doubt that she was doing the right thing.

"I was in the bathroom and because I was alone, I had this habit of never closing the bathroom door," she explains. "Well, I was in there for only a few minutes when, all of a sudden, the bathroom door slammed shut, like someone had given it a good push, and when I tried to get it open it wouldn't budge. So I was trapped in the bathroom."

She was scared, she remembers.

"I didn't have a phone with me and even though I pushed and pushed, it just would not open," she says. "Finally, I just gave it one big push and it flew open, but I was terrified. There was no one else in the apartment with me and, strangely enough, the lock in the doorknob wasn't locked. But now, when I think about what happened, it was almost like someone or something was standing on the other side of the door preventing me

18

from opening it. I know. Crazy, right? But truthfully, that's exactly what it seemed like. I was scared to death and from that point on, I closed the door when I was in the bathroom."

Her friends and family said the door must have blown shut and became jammed, "But I can guarantee you there was no wind in the apartment that day. There is absolutely no way that door blew shut ... no way." She adds.

And why couldn't she get the door to open?

"Well," she says, "That's another question that I can't answer."

When she finally gave the landlord her notice, Carrie says the woman didn't say anything except that she was sorry to see her move out because she was a good tenant.

"But she knew," Carrie says. "She knew why I had to move out and she didn't try to convince me to stay. Clearly, she had been through this situation many times before."

Does she now believe in ghosts?

"Absolutely," she nods.

"They're real," she says. "I know that now. I would never again dismiss what anyone ever says about ghosts."

And getting back to her mother's fears about this alleged haunted house, Carrie says that sometime after she had moved out of the apartment, she finally told her mom of all the strange experiences she had in the place.

"She didn't say anything like 'I told you so,' " Carrie says. "Instead, she explained that when she was a youngster she had heard stories about the house, which had been sitting empty at that time, being haunted. In typical childhood fashion, she didn't believe anything of what she heard, until one summer evening when she and her cousin were riding their bikes past the house and, as they stopped to look at the place, like curious kids will do, they saw a man looking at them from a second story window."

Pausing, Carrie adds, "Guess which window that was? If you guessed the window that was in the bedroom where I saw the man that night standing at the foot of my bed, you were correct."

She says if her mother had told her that story before she had rented the apartment, she's not sure she would have ever moved in.

"You know, I don't think I would have," she says. "That might have been the one thing that would have kept me out of that place … but I can pretty much guarantee you that I won't be going back in there any time soon."

There's a Ghost in the House

It is believed that this is the grave of Hal Mailman. It is located high on a hill that overlooks the house that Kim Lawson says is haunted.

Remember, as a child when you thought every old house in your neighbourhood must be haunted?

Sure you do. In fact, we've all likely experienced those feelings of trepidation at some point in our lives, but very few of us have ever had those feelings confirmed because, as we like to tell ourselves, there are no such thing as ghosts and haunted houses. Or is there? For Kim Lawson and her family, who live in an historic home located in the seaside village of Port Mouton, Queens County, those feelings have not only been confirmed but they've been reaffirmed many times over.

"There's no question in my mind that our house is haunted," Kim says matter of factly, and without hesitation.

She notes that the property, where their century-old home sits, has been occupied for several centuries, and, that in fact, their current home was built on the foundation of a much older residence that had burned down.

"So, I should not be surprised to think that our house would have ghosts, and I'm not," she insists, adding that she and her family have had so many unexplained experiences in their home that they've learned to take it all in stride.

"We're really not afraid of whoever is haunting our house," she says. "Sometimes it can be a little unsettling to think you share your house with spirits, but after a while you just learn to take it all in stride."

Her first memories of paranormal activity at her house go back to when she was a child and her parents owned the home.

"I can remember, as a little girl, sitting at the kitchen table and hearing footsteps as if someone had come in through the back door," she recalls. "Then we would hear a latch lift up and a trap door opening, and that was followed by more footsteps, as if they were going down into a cellar."

Only, Kim points out, their house didn't have a cellar.

However, she explains that her father told the kids that what they were hearing were the footsteps of the former owner, an old man named Hal Mailman who lived in the first house that had been built on the existing foundation and that, in fact, there had been a storage basement in the old house where Hal kept his wood.

"We were young," Kim says. "So of course those stories were scary to us at first, but as we got older, we just took them in stride, and whenever we heard those kinds of noises we'd just shrug and joke about old Hal coming to visit. Footsteps and creaking stairs were common throughout the years. Especially at night," she explains. "You can lay in bed at night and hear someone walking up and down the stairs but no matter when you look, you never see anyone. And I don't care what anyone says, it wasn't the house settling. I know what that sounds like."

The house is haunted, she is sure about that. That point was driven home to her many years later after she had grown up, gotten married and started having children of her own. By that time, she and her husband Gary had taken over the home and her parents had moved out. She remembers one incident in particular when she was getting one of the bedrooms ready for the arrival of her first baby, and her own mother, who lived next door, had come over to help her paint.

"We were painting away in the nursery," she says, "when the radio that we kept in the master bedroom just down the hallway all of sudden just started playing. I mean, it was out of the blue and we have no idea how it started because there was no one else in the house that day except for me and Mom, and we were both in the nursery, so I know neither of us had done it."

Regardless, Kim says her mother went into the larger room and turned off the radio, then returned to the nursery to continue painting.

"She wasn't there long before the radio came back on again," Kim says, adding that her mother quickly went back to the room one more time and switched off the radio. "We were completely baffled because there was no way that radio could come on by itself, yet there it was."

A few minutes later, Kim says, it happened again and this time both she and her mother went to the other room to investigate.

"The really strange thing about this," she shrugs, "was that when we checked things out, we discovered that not only wasn't there anyone else in the house who would be turning the radio on, but, in fact, the radio wasn't even plugged in and there was no battery backup." How that could happen, Kim says, remains a mystery to this very day.

But mysteries are common in their house.

"Strange things happen all the time in this house, like getting up in the morning and finding water and cereal dumped all over the kitchen floor," she explains. "Since it was only me and Gary in the house at the time, we had no idea how that could happen as I'm sure neither of us would be responsible for such a prank. I didn't do it, and I'm sure Gary didn't do it, so how the mess got there, I have no idea."

She also recalls a strange incident that occurred during one of their first Christmases at the house.

"It was Christmas Eve," Kim begins, noting that Gary was asleep in the upstairs bedroom when she went down to the kitchen to get a drink of water.

"To get to the kitchen," she explains, "we had to come down the stairs and go through the living room, passing the Christmas tree along the way. So that's what I did. I went and had my drink but on the way back, as I passed the tree, I could hear a music box playing and it was playing the song 'What a Wonderful World.' I love that song and I remember thinking how nice it was that Gary had bought me a music box for Christmas that played one of my favourite songs."

Putting the incident out of her head, Kim went back up stairs and back to bed. The next morning, after the presents were all opened, she asked Gary if he had changed his mind about giving her the music box and he looked at her dumbfounded. He had no idea what she was talking about and insisted he had not bought her a music box. But she knows what she heard and it wasn't until years later that she finally figured out the truth behind that mystery.

"However," she says, "there were a lot more strange incidents to come for them at this house. For example, my young nephew who was three or four at the time was staying with us one night when he woke up screaming and crying. We could tell he was terrified but no matter how hard we tried we could never get him to tell us what had happened. Whatever happened to him that night I have no idea, but I'm sure it had something to do with the ghosts," Kim says. "A young kid who wasn't used to that sort of thing would be terrified of some of these things. Who wouldn't be? I know of many adults who wouldn't stay in our house either."

Over the years, she says they've experienced lights going on and off, smoke alarms sounding for no reason (even when the batteries were removed), the sounds of someone running up and down the stairs, doors opening and closing, smells of a pipe, tobacco and coffee, and cupboard doors slamming shut as if someone were looking for something.

"But we've learned to live with all of that," she says, "however, there was one incident several years ago that left me shaken. It happened around 4:30 in the morning. I was awoken by the sounds of little girls giggling and the unmistakable sounds of someone riding a tricycle. I was sure it was coming from the living room."

So up she got, being careful not to wake Gary or the children, and made her way down the stairs to the livingroom. When she got there, the noises had stopped.

"I heard them," Kim insists. "I am absolutely sure about that, but I looked everywhere that night and couldn't find anything in the house to explain what I heard."

Although she went back to bed, she says she had trouble sleeping that night and a few days later when she was telling her mother about the incident, she was surprised by her mother's response.

"My mother grew up in this house," Kim says. "She had two sisters, one of which was confined to a wheelchair and who was deceased by the time of this incident. Mom told me that she and her other remaining sister would often push their disabled sister around the living room in her wheelchair, and the thing she remembered other than her sister laughing and giggling, was that the wheels squeaked and she is sure that they would have sounded a lot like a tricycle."

The other thing her mother remembered about her deceased sister was that she liked music boxes. It all made sense to Kim. She was relieved to finally have some answers that she felt she could accept.

But no matter what happened at their house, Kim insists she never felt threatened or intimidated in any way.

"I can honestly say that even though I am one hundred per cent certain that my house is haunted, I have never once been afraid of this place," she says. "Some strange things have happened here, I'll give you that much, but I have never been scared to stay here. I've been a little shocked at times by some of the stuff that happens here, but never afraid."

"Haunted or not," she adds, "This is my house and I would not let anyone or any spirit make me feel uncomfortable in my own house."

The Hand

Dan, who lives in a small community in the Annapolis Valley, not far from Kentville, never believed in ghosts.

He had heard about them as a youngster because, as he puts it, how could anyone grow up in Nova Scotia and not hear such stories? Folklore has always been part of his family life, but he admits that he never bought into superstitions.

He always dismissed those happenings as just that—stories, devised by an over- active imagination or based on fears that had no basis in fact. Not that he didn't think that some people actually believed their own stories, but he just didn't buy into the idea that ghosts could possibly exist.

Today, however, he concedes that's a different story.

"Yes," he nods. "I most certainly do believe."

And for good reason he insists, adding that following an experience he had several years ago, he never again will dismiss anyone's beliefs, even those that may seem far-fetched to reasonably thinking people.

"I've changed my thinking on ghosts," Dan explains.

He notes that even though he now appreciates the stories that others share about their encounters with the paranormal, he also accepts that there are many people who thought just as he did. So for that reason, he is reluctant to give his full identity, but he insists that what he is about to tell us actually happened.

"Yes," he insists as he begins his tale about his encounter with the paranormal. "It's real and it really did happen."

It was an early fall day, September 7, 2001, when he had an experience that changed his life forever, an experience that finally convinced him once and for that ghosts are real.

"It was shortly after 9:30 that evening and I was walking home from a friend's house. I had to take a road that was reputed to be haunted but I was okay with that because I didn't believe in ghosts," he says with a nervous chuckle. "As a kid growing up in this area, I had heard all the stories about there being a ghost of an old woman who supposedly haunted that road, but I admit that I didn't believe any of them. The story went that the old woman had lived in a house that used to be located there, but it eventually burned down several years after she died. I don't know how she died, but as a kid, we were told the old woman roams the road looking for her house."

Dan explains that as youngsters they avoided the area.

"The story went that if she caught you, then she would carry you into the woods and you'd never be seen again," he says. "But I can honestly say that we never heard of anyone going missing."

Dan doesn't know anything about the woman—who she was, where she came from, how she died or even if she really existed—but he says the story of her existence became the stuff of legend around the town where he lived.

"But kids are susceptible to such things and we were terrified of the stories we heard about the ghost and none of us would travel that road for fear of encountering the old woman who walked there," Dan says. "As we got older, though, and became braver, we began travelling that road more often, but most of the kids in my neighbourhood still wouldn't travel alone. They would only travel in groups because, I guess, they figured if there was more than one of them, then the old woman wouldn't bother them."

As for Dan, however, he didn't believe in ghost stories so he didn't allow the fear to rule his life.

"I was too cool to be afraid of ghosts," he reflects. "Most teenage boys I know would never allow their true feelings to show. So when it came time to walk home from my friend's house that September night, I put on a brave face and headed out the door."

About ten or fifteen minutes into the walk, he came to the section of road that was dark and void of any houses, which meant he would have to go the next leg of the walk only by moonlight.

"Thank God it was a clear night and the moon and stars were out," he says. "At least they put out enough light to let me see the road in front of me. It wasn't long before I wished I had brought a flashlight with me, but I didn't have one, so I had no choice but to keep on going. Besides, I knew I was about halfway home so there's no way I was going to turn around and go back to my friend's house."

It wasn't long, however, before Dan say he wished he had stayed at his friend's house and called his dad to come and pick him up, even if it meant his father might not appreciate being bothered.

"Because, honestly, what happened next scared me half to death and forever changed the way I think about ghosts. It also got me thinking that maybe, just maybe, some of those stories that we hear may be more factual than we would like to think or care to admit," Dan says. "A change of attitude came about as I travelled along that dark, deserted stretch of road that September night. I was just walking along minding my own business when it suddenly felt like I wasn't alone anymore," he explains. "Ever have one of those feelings when you think that someone is watching you but when you look around, you see there's no one there? Well, that's exactly how I felt."

Dan adds that in fact, as he quickened his pace, the feelings became all the more intense until he finally stopped in the middle of the road, turned in a complete circle and yelled out to see if anyone was there.

"I actually called out to see if anyone answered," he says. "Of course, even though I didn't think I believed in ghosts, the first thing that ran through my mind were the stories that I had heard of the ghost of the old woman who supposedly haunted the road—the very some road he was now on, alone and in the dark. I'll admit that it was right at that moment that I suddenly felt scared," he says. "There's brave and then there's stupid and I'd have to be pretty stupid not to be afraid then, because the more I stood in that spot looking around, the more intense the feelings became and I was convinced that I was being watched."

Dan says he has no idea how long he stood there in the middle of the road, frozen in his tracks, but he eventually came to his senses when he heard the unmistakable rustling sounds of someone stomping through the thick bushes that were growing at the side of the road.

"Could it have been someone else? Yes I suppose, but who would be there at that time of the night? Could it have been a dog or another animal? Of course," he says, "but the truth was he was beginning to think it was time to get the heck out of that place. The final cue to move came a few seconds later when—and I swear this is true—I saw a hand coming from the bushes." He pauses and swallows hard before he continues. "I swear to God and on everything that I hold dear to me, I saw a hand moving toward me from the bushes. I didn't see anything else. No body, no head, no face, no nothing. Just a hand."

But, that's all he needed to see, because in that split second he turned and quickly kicked his feet into high gear.

"I don't know what it was," he says. "And quite honestly, I wasn't sticking around long enough to see what it was."

Today, talking about his experiences, Dan admits that he could have been so worked up by what he thought he felt that he could have allowed his imagination to get the best of him, but then he adds, "I don't think so. It could have been the result of an over-active imagination, but I've thought about this event many times over the years and I'm convinced that that hand was real."

He's not saying the hand belonged to any ghostly woman who supposedly roamed that stretch of road in search of unsuspecting victims, but what else would it have been?

What else, indeed?

The Lady on the Lake

Mysterious sightings of a woman in white on and around Darling Lake near Yarmouth have led to the Legend of the Lady on the Lake.

Darling Lake is located on the Evangeline Trail, which is actually the main highway route No.1, and is situated 15 kilometres northeast from the old seaport town of Yarmouth, Nova Scotia.

The lake is named after Colonel Michael Ashley Darling, who, in the late 18th century, was sent to Yarmouth to inspect the newly formed militia stationed there. The young colonel was so impressed with the beauty and peacefulness of the spot that he named it Darling Lake.

Today, those who study paranormal occurrences in Nova Scotia believe that because of its strategic location, the lake is a hotbed of ghostly activity. A mathematically devised pattern of lines, spread out across the province, called "lay lines" have been of great interest to many researchers and authors who theorize that an unusual amount of energy can be detected where the lines intersect.

These points of intersection include the communities of New Ross, Mount Uniacke and McGowan Lake, all places where unusual paranormal experiences are known to have occurred over the years. Like these other places, a vortex is located around Darling Lake, and some observers believe that explains the ghostly phenomena experienced there.

Stories of a woman being seen on and around the lake go way back many decades. Over the years, there have been many reports of the Lady on the Lake and those who have seen her have been touched by her appearance as they insisted it was an ethereal experience. Most witnesses say the experience leaves them with an overwhelming feeling of sadness and foreboding.

One of the most believable stories happened several years ago, in the mid-1990s, at about 2:30 early one morning when two men were heading back toward Yarmouth. The pair, who was driving in a truck heading in the direction of Yarmouth, was forced to stop all of a sudden when they saw what they now refer to as the Lady on the Lake.

As the men came around a bend in the road near the lake, they both saw a young woman with long, flowing white hair wearing a long, white dress and standing in the middle of the road. The driver slammed on the brakes, but the vehicle couldn't stop in time and plowed into the woman. Both men thought they had run into the woman and were afraid that they had killed her, but they also felt it was strange that they had not heard a "thump" or felt anything like what they would expect from hitting someone.

Grabbing flashlights, the men quickly got out of the truck and searched around both sides of the road, looking for the woman they were sure they had just run over, but they couldn't find anything.

The men were shaken up pretty badly as they were both convinced that they had seen this mysterious young woman, and they both insisted that they had run into her with the truck, but they were never able to find her. The incident remained a mystery to them.

Two years later, the man who had been driving the truck at the time of the first incident reported seeing the woman again as he was passing the lake. This time he saw her near the lake, and he knew it was the same woman because she was dressed in a long white dress and had long hair that was more white than blonde. By the time he got the truck stopped and got out of the vehicle, she was gone. After that, he was convinced the lake was haunted.

Others have seen the woman in white. One witness reported seeing a woman several years ago floating over the water as she crossed from one shore to the other.

"It was like she was walking on water," the woman says. "The strange thing about it though, other than the fact that she was floating on the lake surface, was that even though there was a strong wind blowing that night, her hair and dress were not moving. It was as if the wind was not having any effect on her. The experience just left me feeling sad, as if something tragic had happened to this woman or someone she loved. I had the strange sensation that she was looking for someone."

Another witness reports seeing a woman in a long white, flimsy gown-like dress hovering over the lake one evening as she was driving toward Yarmouth and like the other witnesses, she too was left with a deep feeling of sorrow.

"It was a bit foggy that evening, so I thought at first I was seeing things, but then her image became very distinct and I could see that it was really a woman," the witness says. "I actually pulled the car over to the shoulder of the road, got out and went to the bushes where I watched her. She had long, light coloured hair and she was hovering over the middle of the lake."

While the witness says the apparition only appeared for "maybe" a minute, the woman disappeared just as quickly as she appeared.

"But it wasn't the fog," she insists. "I know what I saw and I know it was the Lady on the Lake. It was pretty creepy, I'll say that much, and it left me feeling sad for her."

So the question is, who is this mysterious Lady on the Lake?

Although there have been numerous reported sightings over the years of this woman in white wandering around Darling Lake, no one knows for sure and today her identity remains a mystery.

Ghosts at the Cooper's Inn

The beautiful and historic Cooper's Inn in Shelburne is reputed to be haunted. A female apparition has often been seen in a side window located on the second level overlooking the barrel factory.

If you live anywhere on the South Shore of Nova Scotia you have probably heard tales of haunted houses, random happenings, and ghost ships that appear and then disappear as quickly as they came. Tales of the unexplained and the inexplicable are common among the residents of this province and in most small towns, such as those found in Shelburne, where the stories have become the stuff of local legend.

Built in 1784, in the aftermath of the American Revolution, as pro-British refugees flooded into Shelburne, the original vertical log structure, known today as The Cooper's Inn, served as both store and home to a remarkable blind man named George Gracie.

In 1785, Gracie was a refugee merchant from Boston and was to become one of two representatives of Shelburne County in the Nova Scotia House of Assembly.

During restoration in 1987-88, it was found that the inn was built in two stages—the north side was built first, and is where the owners' apartments are located today. The south side complex followed that section. Stories have it that the north side, with its vertical log walls, was floated up from Boston in George Gracie's ship the Experiment and assembled, with the south side being added at that time.

The smaller building at the rear of the main house was used as a cooperage from about 1904 until 1917 when Chandley Smith built a new barrel factory across the street. That's where barrels are still made today. The old cooperage now houses four rooms all with private baths, two upstairs and two on the ground level, with one that opens onto the breezeway and the other onto the garden.

After her first visit to Shelburne in 2001, Pat Dewar knew she had found a community she would love to call home. With many years in the tourism and hospitality business under her belt, she and her husband purchased The Cooper's Inn in 2005.

Over the years, Pat has incorporated 21st century comforts while at the same time maintaining the historical integrity of the building. While the building has changed hands many times over the years, she says the personal experiences that guests and residents have had at The Cooper's Inn have not. For some visitors, those experiences include an encounter with the resident ghost.

"But it's a friendly ghost," Pat quickly points out, "anyone who has told me about an encounter with the specter also insists that they do not feel intimidated or frightened in any way."

Over the years, she says she has heard many different stories about the ghost at the inn, but she has never personally experienced any such phenomena herself.

"Never," she chuckles. "But I believe that either you are sensitive to these things or you are not and I guess I am not, but we've had many guests who tell us their experiences as well as people who have lived here in the past, and in a lot of cases these experiences are very similar, suggesting that they are more than just coincidence."

For example, Pat tells the story of former residents who had a daughter and she seemed to be sensitive to whatever was going on in the home.

"Every night, when the mother put her daughter to bed, she would tuck her in. After the little girl fell off to sleep and the mother went back into the room to check on things, she'd find that the blankets were often pulled tightly up to the little girl's chin," Pat says. "The next morning, when the mother asked her daughter who tucked her the previous night, the little girl would tell her that it was the lady who was in the room with her."

Pat adds that there was never any other woman in the room, or at least none that anyone else could see. But she says she isn't surprised to hear about a woman in the inn, because most of the stories they hear about ghosts involve a woman.

For instance, she says, "A female apparition has often been seen in a side window overlooking the barrel factory. She has been described as being very tall and slender, and is reported to be standing very stoically and sometimes with a towel draped over her arm."

Whatever is going on at The Cooper's Inn, a female plays prominently in the story. Pat says that she was told of one gentleman who walked into a second floor room and saw a tall, female apparition standing directly in the middle of the room.

"Apparently, she turned and looked right at him," Pat says. "As far as I know, no one has ever been able to identify the woman who roams the rooms and hallways of the inn. But I did once have a woman visitor who was supposedly sensitive to these things and she told me that the name Anna Marie kept coming to her. Coincidently, the name of George Gracie's wife was Anna Marie."

She says there is more evidence to suggest that the spirit that haunts the inn is that of a female.

"Our guests will often hear footsteps on the stairs at night as well as a swishing sound that you hear with a long dress," Pat explains. "Only, even though you might wait for someone to turn up at the top of the stairs, no one ever does. But most of the witnesses say that undeniably the sounds reminded them of a woman. As well, it seems this spirit likes to bake bread," she laughs. "We've had guests who reported smelling bread baking throughout the night. They sometimes come down in the morning and compliment me for staying up all night and baking breads for my guests ... only it wasn't me and there was no bread, but Anna Marie was said to be a good cook.

She also likes to clean, Pat quickly adds.

"In another of these stories we've heard about a young girl who was staying here and when she woke up, she watched as an apparition hovered around the room as if cleaning or straightening up. She appears to be very organized and tidy, and likes to have everything in its place. I would love to meet this ghost because she appears to be as proud of her home as I am but I've never had the pleasure."

However, the hauntings are not all about women.

"We've had guests staying here who've told us that they were kept awake all night by the sounds of people running up and down the stairs and pounding their feet and to them, it sounded like the heavy footsteps you would expect to hear from a man," she says. "As well, some of our housekeepers have reported some experiences where it felt like someone was present or was watching them, but no one was there. In most of these cases, the workers reported that it felt like a man was present."

Whether it's a male or female spirit, Pat says the ghost does have a mischievous side to it.

"It's been known to be playful," she says. "Over the years, we've had reports from guests and employees about things going missing or being moved around, from one place to another. Sometimes, things have gone missing for days at a time only to turn up in places you'd least expect to find them."

Regardless, though, Pat says she believes the spirit is harmless.

"No one ever reports being afraid at the inn," she insists. "There is never any fear or intimidation associated with the spirit. In fact, most people say they feel very comfortable around the spirit or spirits."

As for herself, she says, "I can't say I've ever felt anything but at peace here. In fact, it's like this place fits me like a comfortable slipper."

Pat also points out that those visitors who have heard about their ghost often ask for the room that is haunted and they often say they they hope to meet the woman who has been seen at the inn.

"Some people are lucky in that they experience such an encounter," she says. "Others, on the other hand, go away without being as lucky, but vowing they will return in the hopes of one day seeing the ghost of The Cooper's Inn."

The Hand on the Rock

It was the second worst air disaster in Canadian history. There were no survivors among the 215 passengers and 14 crewmembers en route from New York to Geneva. The flight took off from JFK International Airport on September 2, 1998 at 9:18 p.m. local time. It carried a Saudi Arabian prince, well-known scientists, a renowned AIDS activist, United Nations officials, newlyweds, mothers, fathers, brothers, sisters, sons and daughters. Two Canadians were among those who died aboard Flight 111.

The three-engine McDonnell Douglas MD-11 was travelling at approximately 33,000 feet when it passed over Liverpool, at 10:22 p.m. At that time, the crew notified air traffic control in Moncton, New Brunswick, that there was smoke in its cockpit. Captain Urs Zimmermann and First Officer Stephan Loew requested an unscheduled landing suggesting Boston, but were diverted to Halifax because it was closer, only 70 nautical miles compared to 300.

According to air traffic control recordings released after the tragedy by the Transportation Safety Board of Canada, when the crew learned a few minutes later that it was only 30 miles to the runway, they informed air traffic control that they needed more distance. The plane was still travelling at between 15,000 and 18,000 feet. At that point, Flight 111 turned toward the north, then announced that it needed to dump fuel before it could land. The MD-11 has a maximum landing weight of 200,000 tonnes and the plane at that point weighed 230,000 tonnes due to the additional fuel needed to get to Europe.

With directions from air traffic control, Flight 111 continued its turn and headed south over St. Margaret's Bay on the southern coast of Nova Scotia, preparing to dump fuel. At 10:24 p.m. the crew radioed: "We are declaring an emergency. . . . we have to land immediately."

That was the last communication from Flight 111. Radar tracked the aircraft for a further six minutes as it turned toward the west, then completed a 360-degree orbit into a southeast direction and disappeared. Residents all along the South Shore reported hearing a low-flying aircraft followed by a reverberating bang. Some people on the Aspotogan Peninsula near Blandford and Chester reported that a crash had shaken their homes around 10:30 p.m.

Local fishermen were the first to take to the water to search for the downed passenger plane, quickly followed by the RCMP, Coast Guard, military ships and aircraft. The search continued until debris was subsequently located about eight kilometres southwest of the world-famous Peggy's Cove, a few kilometres off the small island of East Ironbound around 12:30 a.m. the next morning.

At its peak, nine navy and five coast guard vessels, led by HMCS Preserver, were in the St. Margaret's Bay area. Over 1,500 soldiers, sailors and airmen were involved in the recovery effort, along with the RCMP, other government agencies and volunteers, including local ground search and rescue teams. Hundreds of other volunteers provided everything from grief counselling to boxed lunches.

Forty Transportation Safety Board investigators worked on the Flight 111 disaster along with about 380 RCMP officers who were divided between recovery and victim identification efforts. Investigators looked into all aspects of the crash, reviewed information on aircraft specifications and maintenance, along with human performance by the crew and all those associated with Flight 111. But it is information gleaned from the flight data recorder and cockpit voice recorder, the famous black boxes that helped investigators the most.

The flight data recorder, which maintains records of more than 100 parameters associated with the plane's operation, was recovered two days after the crash, and flown to a Transportation Safety Board lab in Ottawa. But it was announced the following day that it had stopped recording at 10,000 feet giving no information about the last six minutes of Flight 111.

In March 2003, a report from the Transportation Safety Board concluded that when a fire started in the ceiling above the cockpit, the 229 people on board the jet had no chance of survival. That conclusion came with the release of the board's final report into the disaster. More than 300 pages detail the series of dangers and deficiencies on the MD-11 that made it impossible for the pilots to have any chance of landing safely.

The crash site was eight kilometres from the shore, not far from Peggy's Cove. A short walking trail to a monument in memory of the people who lost their lives can be found at the Swissair Memorial Site in Peggy's Cove in the South Shore region.

Following the crash, two memorials to those who died were established by the Government of Nova Scotia to honour the victims. One is to the east of the crash site at a place known as The Whalesback, approximately one kilometre north of Peggy's Cove. The second memorial is a more private, but much larger commemoration, located west of the crash site near Bayswater Beach Provincial Park on the Aspotogan Peninsula in Bayswater. Here, the unidentified remains of the victims are interred.

So this is the background to this story. Now we move ahead to April 15, 2012 when Liverpool residents Camden Bishop Shot, Reagan Shot and their mom, Kendra Shot, got up early in the morning and headed off to go to Halifax to get some summer clothes.

"It was really foggy that day when we left," Camden recalls. "We left Halifax around supper time to return home. We were just before the Hammonds Plains exit when I asked my mom if we could go to Peggy's Cove. I had never been there before and it was a place I always wanted to visit."

Upon their arrival at the popular tourist destination, the trio first went to the famed Peggy's Cove lighthouse and gift shop, but as it was getting ready too close, they only had time for a quick look around. From there, they decided to visit the Swissair Memorial at Whalesback.

"When we got there my mom told my brother Reagan and me to be respectful, and not to fight, because we were in a sacred place and we need to respect it," Camden recalls. "She also told us that we had to remain on the path and not go off it. The whole time I was taking pictures with my iPad as we walked down the eerie path. It was very foggy and you could hardly see out over the water. It felt strange."

When they got to the end of the path, they paused to view the two monuments that had been erected to remember the crash victims and he says he remembers thinking that the place seemed eerily quiet and still.

"My mom and I took separate pictures of each of the monuments," he recalls. "I was finished taking photos of the one on the right so I tried to take some photos of the ocean and that's when I accidentally stepped off the path."

At that point, he says his mom turned around to take a picture of the monument and she asked who had touched the rock.

"I turned around and there was a handprint on the rock," Camden says. "It hadn't been there earlier and I was sure that I had not touched it nor did my mom or brother. We concluded this after a short argument. There were no water puddles visible anywhere and nobody else at the monument with us so we had no idea who had made the print."

Camden admits that the sudden appearance of the handprint did scare him but his little brother was not scared at all.

"Mom touched the rock thinking maybe the dew from the fog would allow a wet print if somebody touched the rock," he says. "But it didn't and we have no idea where the print came from. The handprint was smaller than my mom's and larger than mine or my little brother's, so we knew it wasn't from any of us. I cannot explain what happened that day, all that I do know is that we were the only people there that day and nobody touched the rock."

The drive home was very quiet, as nobody really knew what to say, Camden recalls.

"When my mom got home we looked over the manifest for the flight that had crashed," he says. "We discovered there were a few teenagers on the plane and they realized that the size of the handprint on the rock was about the size of a teenager's hand. This experience scared me, but my mom tried to reassure me that even though until that day she really did not have a belief in the afterlife or ghosts that somebody was definitely reaching out to us and that they were thanking us for coming to the site to remember them and for me not to be scared," Camden says. "It has definitely changed my outlook on life and the possibility of afterlife."

Ghosts in the Bay

Bedford Basin, in Halifax, is a large enclosed bay, forming the northwestern end of Halifax Harbour. It is named in honour of John Russell, the fourth Duke of Bedford, and it is said to be haunted.

That's right. Over the years, witnesses have reported hearing the apparitional sounds of a rowboat on foggy nights, but no boat ever appears.

Local legend says that many years ago, a dory filled with fisherman overturned in the bay. They now forever try to find their way back to shore, but they never find their way.

'Inn' the spirit

Lunenburg's Arbor View Inn — historic, yes. But haunted?
You be the judge!

When Cindy Sangster purchased the Arbor Inn Bed and Breakfast in Lunenburg back in 2008, she says she fears that she got more than she bargained for. At the time, she says she had no idea that one of the previous owners of the stately, century old, three-story Dufferin Street residence had perhaps left something very personal behind when she died—her spirit.

Located on property that was once known as the Old Robert Lindsay Farm, the house was built in 1907, near the site of what is now Fishermen's Memorial Hospital for Henry Havelock McIntosh.

"His father, Duncan, apparently went to California during the gold rush in the late 1800s more than once and was very successful," Cindy explains. "The family story is that Duncan probably funded the building of this

51

home because Henry was inspector of schools at the time and they didn't make a lot of money."

The story goes that the younger Mr. McIntosh was married twice and fathered five children, his first wife dying in the late 1800s.

The older picture of Annette Hebb-Grier, left, taken in the backyard when she was about three years old reveals a girl who looks like, and is dressed like, an apparition Cindy Sangster's friend Jackie saw in the Inn's kitchen back in September 2011.

"They had a very tragic family, too. One of the sons was, I believe, killed in the First World War and another son came back with a British bride," she explains. "He was a drunkard and a womanizer ... and she didn't like him and wanted to leave with their son Charlie and he wouldn't let her. He came home and threatened her."

He eventually ended up dying accidentally when, in a state of drunkenness, he impaled himself with a knife. Ironically, just prior to that occurring, his wife had taken poison because her husband wouldn't let her leave.

"She didn't die," Cindy says, "but ended up being charged with his murder as a murder-suicide. That was in the springtime, in the early 1930s. She recovered by the fall and got off from the charge because it was discovered to be just circumstance, coincidence, and she went back to England with Charlie."

Henry McIntosh also died in the early 1930s, and in 1935 the home was acquired from the estate by Lawrence Lamont Hebb who bought the property because his wife Marion loved the house so much. While tragedy seemed to follow the McIntoshes during their years residing in the home, such was not the case for the Hebbs.

"Marion raised their family here, their kids, nieces, nephews, it was like the drop-in spot," Cindy explains. "You could always come to grandma's house and hang out."

Mr. Hebb, who went on to become mayor of Lunenburg, died in 1973 at the age of 85. However, Mrs. Hebb lived to the ripe old age of 104 and resided in the house until she was nearly 100. And while she may have died in 1994, it seems Ms. Hebb apparently decided at some point in 2011 to make a curtain call back to the living.

"The first time that anyone mentioned her to me was in September of 2011 and we didn't know who she was

53

then," Cindy says. "There were guests staying in what they called the Annapolis Suite, which is the big suite upstairs."

She recalls that it was a family, Mom and Dad and two kids going to university in Halifax, so they came to Lunenburg for the night. The next morning at breakfast, the mother of the group told her hostess that she and her son had both heard a rocking chair rocking throughout the night.

"I said, 'that's weird, because the only rocking chair is in the parlour, three floors below, and it's a glider, so you wouldn't hear it way up there.'" Cindy says. "I left it at that and everybody packed up to leave," she recalls.

Cindy adds that the mother let the family go out to the car, turned around and closed the door and stood there and looked at her and said she had to tell me that she is a medium. The woman told her that some people don't accept that and are spooked by it, but she had to tell me that there was a rocking chair in her room last night and it was rocking. The guest told Cindy that the sound of the chair was very distinctive and she had no doubt it was that of a wooden rocking chair on wooden floorboards. She also told her hostess that while in the room, some names came to her—Annette, Robbie and Lad— the latter perhaps being a collie dog—and she received a clairvoyant picture of a woman rubbing her tummy and that she was actually pregnant.

Upon later investigation, Cindy learned that Ms. Hebb actually had a daughter named Annette and that she was alive and well and living in Ontario. She contacted the now Annette Hebb-Grier via e-mail and learned even more interesting connections. There was indeed not only one Robbie associated with the family, a young man who at one time worked in her father's Lunenburg Hardware store and in the family garden, but also another—her mother's favourite cousin who went by the name Rob.

As for Lad, Ms. Hebb-Grier did not remember a dog by that name. However "Lad" was her father's nickname when he was a young man growing up in the town.

She also noted that her mother always had a rocking chair, in fact hers was a Lunenburg made "Johnny rocking chair,' but couldn't picture her being upstairs in it on the third floor, although there were other rocking chairs on every floor of the home.

"So whether there's a crossover or a correlation, who knows?" Cindy says.

Three days after her communication with Ms. Hebb-Grier, she received another e-mail from her medium guest that said she was getting even more information, a vision of a woman holding a wooden object with an acorn or a pineapple on top. She also said the presence she felt in the house kept referring to pear trees. When told of this, Ms. Hebb-Grier said she knew of no such wooden object and there were no pear trees on the property, however there were quince, which often can resemble pears that her mother used to make jams and jellies out of those.

While doubters might try and pass off Ms. Hebb's first appearance at the house as a product of a guest's imagination coupled with some very unusual coincidences, it didn't take long for her spirit to show up once again.

One day at the end of that same September, Cindy's friends Christine and Jackie came down for a girls' night to sit on the deck, and apparently Ms. Hebb's apparition thought it might be a nice idea to join them.

"We were coming through the kitchen, out here onto the deck and Christine paused and looked at Jackie, and Jackie looked up the stairs, and they both looked at each other. I asked, 'What,' and they said 'Nothing,' and we came out and sat outside. " she says. "I said, 'What was that about?' and they said, 'Oh, there was a lady on the stairs up there.' I said 'nooooo.' "

Having a hunch as to what her two visitors had seen, Cindy suggested the three take their drinks upstairs to investigate. The three sat down on a couch, looked across the room and almost immediately Christine and Jackie began to rock back and forth.

When asked why they were doing it, the two answered that they didn't know, it was instinctive because there was a lady sitting across from them in a chair, rocking.

Jackie told Cindy, who had grabbed a notebook and started writing down what was happening, that the woman was talking about a collie dog, more white than black, but black through the throat area, and the name was Lad.

"Jackie and Christine could not have known any of this," she says.

Jackie also said the woman talked about a carved, wooden acorn jewelry box with legs, and that there was a blue or green necklace inside. It had a drop in the centre, but it wasn't in the box anymore and no one had the box.

At one point, Cindy says she opened the patio door to let some fresh air in and was told by Jackie to close it as Ms. Hebb doesn't like the door open. She says her unexpected guest was described as wearing a long black dress with a white collar, her black and grey-streaked hair pulled back in a bun.

When they asked her name, Christine received a message that it was Mary "or something like that."

Cindy insists that none of them knew at that point that Ms. Hebb's first name was actually Marion.

At one point, Christine and Jackie also noticed the apparition's hand on her tummy and that she was making the letter "A" with her fingers.

"So we akin that to being Annette, as she was pregnant with Annette when she moved into this house," Cindy says.

Their upstairs encounter that evening lasted about an hour, after which the trio went downstairs and into the kitchen, collectively shaking their heads over what they had just experienced.

"Jackie is standing there, and all of a sudden she says that here used to be cupboards up here ... and there's a little girl standing there—she's got long curly hair, she's got a little flowered dress on, black shoes and white socks," says Cindy.

Cindy went to her office and retrieved a photo that Ms. Hebb-Grier had sent to her, taken when she was three-years-old playing outside the doll house that was in the back yard. The description Jackie had given of the girl she saw in the kitchen matched the photo of Ms. Hebb-Grier perfectly.

"There is no way Jackie would have known about that picture or that there were cupboards where there weren't cupboards anymore," she says. "It was just surreal."

That was the second and last time to date that anything spiritually unusual had happened in the house during Cindy's ownership.

She says she's been wanting to get other mediums to the inn to see if they, too, could detect Ms. Hebb's presence, but to date that has not come to fruition. She adds that no one who has encountered Ms. Hebb's spirit, if that is indeed who is rocking chairs and standing on the stairs, has experienced any "bad vibes" during the experience.

"I've always felt very comfortable in this house, it's got a very warm energy to it," Cindy says. "It's because she's happy here, she's content to be here."

Lunenburg's Arbor View Inn — historic, yes. But haunted? You be the judge!

Haunted Halifax

With its long history of disasters and shipwrecks, it seems like tragedy shrouds the city of Halifax, not unlike the dense fog that often rolls in from its harbour. It should come as a surprise to no one that Halifax has more than its fair share of haunted locations and resident spooks.

One of Halifax's most infamous spooky sites is the Five Fishermen Restaurant and Grill, located on the bustling corner of Carmichael and Argyle streets. Having once served as a mortuary, the 200-year-old structure is, perhaps, one of the more famous haunted spots in the city.

The four-story, brick-and-wood building opened in 1816 as a schoolhouse, and was eventually taken over by a local family and turned into a funeral home. Victims of two significant disasters of the 20th century — the sinking of the Titanic off Newfoundland in April 1912 and the Halifax Explosion of 1917, were brought to this location where they remained until they were either claimed by family or eventually buried.

Considering this history then, it's only natural that the Five Fishermen would be considered "haunted." Over the years, reports of flying silverware, and arguing voices, after the doors have been locked for the night, abound.

An elderly gentleman in a long black coat is often seen walking into and through a wall mirror. Two Victorian dressed ladies wander the staircase only to vanish. Cold spots frequent the premises.

But paranormal activity is not new to Halifax. Ghosts have been reported in Halifax since the city was founded, when Colonel Edward Cornwallis and 2,600 settlers climbed upon its shores in 1749. However, perhaps some of the more intriguing stories are a direct result of the explosion of 1917.

A head in silhouette, on the third window of the St. Paul's Anglican church, shines as a haunting reminder of one of the most devastating man-made explosions in human history. Several streets up the steep hills sits the former Victoria General Hospital, where many of the wounded were cared for. There is it said, a grey nun wanders the halls in search of the dying.

In 1917, Halifax Harbour was a bustling hub of activity where ships, troops and supplies were gathered and transported to Europe as part of the Second World War effort. The city's population had grown in relation to that effort, with many moving to Halifax to take advantage of the prosperity war often offers.

The morning of December 6 was no different than any other typical morning — boats were being loaded and unloaded, children walked to school, businesses opened for the day, and trains ran on time.

At 7:30 a.m., both the French freighter Mont Blanc and the Norwegian ship Imo weighed anchor from the Bedford Basin heading for The Narrows and points beyond. The Mont Blanc was loaded with a volatile mix of wet and dry picric acid, TNT, gun cotton, and benzol; bound for the European arena. The Imo under ballast was destined for New York.

At approximately 8:40 a.m., they collided, as the Imo struck the bow of the Mont Blanc. Fire broke out immediately on the French freighter. The captain and crew, fearing an imminent explosion, took to lifeboats and rowed to the Dartmouth side of the harbour.

The Mont Blanc burned for 20 minutes and came to rest by Pier 6 of Halifax's north end. Curious at the unusual sight, many stopped to observe, unaware of the boat's dangerous cargo. Between 9:04 and 9:05 a.m., she exploded and disintegrated into fragments decimating population and property both near and far.

Almost 2,000 people died, well over 4,000 were maimed and injured, 1,630 buildings were reduced to rubble, and 12,000 were damaged. Windows rattled up and down the distant shores of the province. While Halifax already had her share of ghost stories, they would grow to legendary proportions after the explosion.

One of the most popular ghost explosion stories is actually quite visible to anyone walking down Argyle Street. Upon closer examination of St. Paul's Church, the oldest Protestant church in Canada, you can see the silhouette of a man's head in a window.

The story goes that even though the window has been changed several times since the explosion in an attempt to banish the shadowy reminder, every time it reappears in the new glass as if the old building refuses to allow the city to forget.

There are several different stories that attempt to explain the silhouette's existence in the window. The most popular story, which is told in a local walking ghost tour, is the tale of a young organist practicing in the church at the time of the explosion. It is said the young man was decapitated in the explosion and his head blasted

This silhouette of a man seems to be forever engraved on a window in Halifax's historic St. Paul's Church.

through the window, leaving behind the silhouette as a constant reminder of the tragedy.

Another story states that it is the head of one of the hapless sailors from ground zero. And yet a further tale says the silhouette bears a remarkable likeness to the Reverend Jean-Baptiste Moreau who served as an assistant to the church. It is said the reverend was standing in the window at the time of the explosion and the resulting flash forever seared his image into the holy glass.

Whoever the head belongs to, the image offers a haunting reminder of that terrible disaster that impacted so many lives all those years ago.

Further up South Street is the location of a former hospital where a little known tale originated from the oldest part of the complex on Tower Road — the former Victoria General. Built in 1867, the doors remained opened for many years to heal and care until it was closed and removed to make way for a new, modern health care facility.

It is said that within the halls of the old hospital wandered the grey nun, an apparition observed by many nurses through the years. She was thought to be a victim of the Halifax Explosion who came to work in the hospital during the Second World. Since her untimely death, she was said to comfort and guide the dying during their final minutes. While administering to her charge, a soft grey light and the faint smell of incense accompanies her.

Today, even though the building is gone, the legend still remains and some even suggest that the grey nun can still be seen around the property — but only when she wants to be seen.

When the first Europeans set foot in what is now Nova Scotia, more than 300 years ago, their arrival changed the course of life for the indigenous inhabitants of this land. Never would their existence be the same.

As settlements grew, European and First Nations cultures clashed. Historic records tell the tale of two peoples trying to coexist in a place where only one had lived and prospered for generations. It was a land rich in natural resources, but still very rugged and raw, and it carried the promise of wealth and prosperity.

Going back in time to the early days of Halifax and the area around Halifax Harbour, we find the story of one Mi'kmaq chief who, having lost one of his daughters to the European traders, decided to take matters into his own hands. When he learned that his daughter had been taken aboard a vessel that had sailed off back to Britain, the chief was furious, so he put a curse on the land. He predicted that three things would happen there over time. The first, he said, would be very violent. The second would be rather quiet, and the third would be long lasting.

Now, in the late 1800s, they built the first bridge, a wooden walkway, across the span from what is now Halifax on one side of the harbour to Dartmouth on the other. It was up for a short time until a violent winter storm brought it crashing down. A few years later, the settlers replaced it with a railway bridge. It was up for some time, then, on a very quiet, calm summer evening, it fell. There was no explanation for its collapse.

In 1955, when the MacDonald Bridge was being built, the builders were smart enough to ask the Mi'kmaq chief at the time to come dispel the curse, pacify the area and bring peace to the land. The chief came and chanted a few chants. That bridge is still standing today.

Even more intriguing than that story is the tale of a little-known piece of joint Canadian-American history. Located in the centre of the city, at the corner of Spring Garden Road and Barrington Street, is the Old Burying Ground, the oldest cemetery in Halifax and a national historic site. Used by all denominations, the Old Burying Ground served the early settlers of Halifax from 1749 until its closure in 1844.

It is estimated that there are somewhere in the vicinity of 1200 head and footstones within the burying ground. Some historians suggest there are more than 10,000 people buried there because in the early days of settlement, the city suffered through epidemics of both typhoid and yellow fever. With so many people dying so quickly, the bodies had to be disposed of immediately. There was little time for fancy, expensive funerals.

Besides, many of the thousands of people believed to be buried there were poor and could not afford an elaborate sendoff to the afterworld, let alone a costly grave marker. In fact, the Halifax debtors' prison was close by, which made the cemetery a convenient place to dispose of its deceased.

Photo by Vernon Oickle

Over the years, witnesses have reported seeing the ghost of Major-General Robert Ross, who is buried in the middle crypt, roaming the historic Old Burying Ground in Halifax.

Within the Old Burying Ground, there is a section set aside for the military. At that location are crypts, raised graves and fancy monuments dedicated to the brave souls that rest there. One of those graves is the final resting place of Major-General Robert Ross.

Robert Ross was a British army officer who participated in both the Napoleonic Wars and the War of 1812. He was born in Rostrevor, County Down, now Northern Ireland. After the defeat of Napoleon, Ross sailed to North America as a major general to take charge of all British troops on the east coast, taking up a post in Halifax.

After the Americans made a daring raid in Toronto, then known as York, during which the invaders burned several government buildings, Ross was sent to personally lead the British troops in the attack on the Americans at the Battle of Bladensburg on August 24, 1814. There, the American army of mostly militia quickly collapsed. Moving on from Bladensburg, Ross captured Washington, D.C. with little resistance. He insisted on only destroying public property, including the U.S. Capitol and the White House.

Based on that success, Ross organized an attack on Baltimore, Maryland. His troops landed at the southern tip of the Patapsco Neck peninsula at North Point, 20 kilometres from the city, on the morning of September 12, 1814. During the march, and just prior to the Battle of North Point, the British troops encountered American skirmishers, and Ross rode forward to personally direct his troops. An American sniper shot him through the right arm into the chest.

According to Baltimore tradition, two American riflemen, teenagers Daniel Wells and Henry McComas, aged 18 and 19 respectively, were credited with killing Ross. Both young men were killed in the engagement. Ross died while being transported back to the ships.

After his death, the general's body was stored in a barrel of 129 gallons of good Jamaican rum and shipped on the British ship HMS Royal Oak to Halifax, where he was buried on September 29, 1814.

But the story doesn't end there. Indeed, it is just the beginning for those who believe in tales of the paranormal. Many witnesses have claimed to see the ghost of Major-General Robert Ross roaming through the Old Burial Ground, his sword drawn for battle as if he is rallying the troops to move on to the next American city.

More haunting experiences wait at one of the city's most recognizable sites, the Halifax Citadel National Historic Site. The British fort, completed in 1856, offers ninety- minute tours exploring every dark nook and cranny where the ghosts of former soldiers are said to lurk.

A steep walk down some 33 stone steps on the southwest demi-bastion leads to a pair of dark, dank rooms with a half-dozen metal cots and grimy, barred windows — a former prison for soldiers.

Over the years, visitors to the site have reported seeing a uniformed man enter a room only to seemingly vanish.

Other sites that are rumoured to be haunted can be found in and around Halifax's historic harbour. Near the waterfront is the Alexander Keith's brewery, which is said to be inhabited by the ghost of the brewmaster himself. McNabs Island, accessible only by boat (ghost ship not required), is reputed to be haunted by the ghost of a former resident who was found drowned.

The Man Upstairs

This is one of the oldest houses in Mill Village, Queens County.
Its owner also says it's haunted.

For some people, the idea that they may be sharing their house with a ghost, would be enough to send them scurrying from the premises, but for others, the notion of living with a wayward spirit who seems trapped between two worlds is actually very exhilarating. They choose to embrace the spirit, thinking it's better to coexist than to try drive it away.

Such is the case of Maude Zwicker, who lives in an historic, centuries' old home in Mill Village, a small hamlet nestled on the banks of the gently flowing Medway River in Queens County on Nova Scotia's South Shore.

Built in 1816 by Samuel Mack, one of the village's original settlers, Maude's house is one of the oldest in the village and was originally used as a tavern to serve the guests of a hotel that was located directly next door to the premises. The road through Mill Village was once

69

originally part of the main route that connected all the settlements along the South Shore and as a midway point the village was a busy spot, not only with the Mack tavern and the hotel next door, but also with several other businesses located in the vicinity at the time including a blacksmith, general store and stables.

Traffic was steady in those early days as people travelled by stagecoach, horseback or horse-drawn carriage so the tavern and hotel had a steady stream of customers and guests. In fact, Maude points out, she believes it was that early stagecoach connection that led to the man being stranded upstairs in her house.

Over time, the home she now owns was sold and was eventually purchased by her grandparents. Maude spent a great deal of her childhood there, she recalls, and enjoyed many youthful adventures on the property.

"I loved the place," she points out.

She adds that she has many fond memories from her childhood years at the house, which she eventually inherited and occupies today. But as a youngster, she wasn't aware that the house came with its own ghost.

"I didn't discover that until one day when I was playing on the staircase landing and my grandmother was down in the kitchen doing whatever she was doing," Maude recalls. "I was playing up there all by myself like a little kid would do and then all of sudden, when I looked up to the top of the stairs, I noticed a man standing there looking back down at me. I was still young, but I remember wondering who he was because I had never seen him in the house before and I knew he wasn't part of the family."

Maude says that the strange thing about this encounter was that even though she had never seen this man before, she was not afraid.

"Maybe I should have been," she shrugs. "After all, I was just a little girl and here was a strange man in our house, but I wasn't. I don't ever remember being afraid of him."

Describing what she saw, Maude says the "man" was roughly in his early to mid- 30s and he was small featured. He was rather short, she says, noting that he appeared to be dressed in a late period suit and a bright white shirt with an old fashioned, button up collar.

He appeared to be the kind of person who was well off financially or some kind of businessman, and she says he looked very nice all dressed in his fine clothing as if he were taking a trip or were on his way to some kind of meeting.

Her theory is that the young man had been a passenger on one of the early stagecoaches and stayed overnight. She suggests that it looks like he was waiting for something so either he missed his ride and he's waiting for the next stagecoach or something bad happened to him while he was there ... something that prevented him from making his connection.

"Even though I have no idea what happened to him or who he was, it could have been that because it looked like he had money, maybe someone robbed him and left him behind as we know things like that happened all the time back then," Maude says. "But whatever happened to this young man, I never once felt frightened or intimidated by the spirit in my grandparents' house. Never. I have encountered him many times over the years as I was growing up and after I moved into the house, I have seen him many times again, but he never comes downstairs to the main level while I'm around. I have seen him many times on the stairs and up on the second floor, but never down on the main floor. I hear him all the time on the second floor, walking around and opening and closing the doors, and sometimes it gets so loud that I have to yell up and tell him to hold it down," Maude says. "And, he does," she laughs. "Maybe he's afraid of me. Other times," she continues, "the cat will sit at the bottom of the staircase for the longest while, just sitting there and watching and looking at something. I can't see it, but it's pretty obvious that the cat sees something. I figure it's probably him—the man upstairs."

But Maude and her cat aren't the only ones who hear and see the ghost.

She recalls an incident several years ago when one of her nieces was visiting the house and was playing on the landing just like she had been when she was younger.

"When I asked my niece what she was doing, she said she was playing with the man," Maude says. "And when I asked her to describe the man for me, she described a man just like I remember. That is more than a coincidence, "Who else would it be?" Maude says.

The Face in the Mirror

It was a rough night, as far as Nancy was concerned. A nurse of seven years, she had just completed her night shift at the local hospital, and after a challenging 12 hours, she was exhausted. The only thing she wanted to do was get home, get out of her uniform and flop into bed. She was so tired, all she could think about was sleeping. She was even too tired to sleep.

She's seen a lot during her time as a nurse, more tragedy and suffering than any human being should have to deal with, but she understands that's part of her profession and she has learned to cope with the emotions that come with the job. But some shifts are worse than others and this recent night shift was one of the worst of her career, highlighted with a fatal motor vehicle accident that claimed the lives of two people.

Having to deal with distraught family members is never easy, she explains, and this incident was particularly tough as the deceased were a mother and her child.

"It was a sad incident — they're all sad and many of them test your faith in God, if you believe in such things," she says. "But this one was especially tough. The mother was only twenty-four and the child was still young, only four. They were involved in a head-on collision when

73

another car crossed the centre line and hit them. I didn't see the accident but I heard it was a real mess."

She says the mother died at the scene but the child was still alive when they pulled him from the wreck. He was in bad shape with serious injuries and Nancy says everyone knew it was doubtful he would survive. In the end, the young boy hung on until he reached the hospital where he died shortly after he arrived in the ER where Nancy works.

"It was one of the hardest things I've ever had to deal with and as a nurse I deal with death all the time, but it's especially difficult when a child is involved," she says. "You feel so bad for the family but there's nothing you can do except to comfort them and what do you say to a young husband and father who has just lost his family? His world just fell apart and there's nothing you can say to comfort him. It was really heartbreaking."

Nancy says she doesn't think she will ever forget the face of that young boy all bloodied and bruised as he lay on the stretcher after the paramedics brought him in, nor will she ever be able to get the father's face out of her mind.

"It broke my heart because you just feel so helpless when you're dealing with something like that. The boy's father was just devastated, but what would you expect? Those images will be there for the rest of my life," she says, "I had contact with the boy and his father. I never came into contact with the deceased woman and that's why the details of what happened after I got home continue to haunt me. It may have been my imagination or my emotions getting the best of me, but I don't think so."

She stresses that what happened while she was in her bathroom getting ready for bed was one of the most bizarre things she has ever experienced.

"I got home and after taking care of the usual personal business, I just couldn't bring myself to go to bed because I knew I wouldn't be able to fall asleep," she says. "Everytime I closed my eyes, all I could see was the broken body of that dear, sweet little boy and the cries from the boy's father kept echoing in my head. It was just terrible so I thought that maybe a nice, long, hot shower might help to relax me."

Nancy says she has no idea how long she was in the shower, but she remembers that when she emerged from the water she couldn't get over how much steam there was in the bathroom.

"There was so much steam in the bathroom that I couldn't see anything," she says. "The mirror was completely obliterated by the steam. Whenever that happens, I usually just wipe the mirror with the bath towel and that's what I did that day," she recalls. "It was difficult keeping the mirror clear because every time I would wipe it dry, it would just fog up again. I think I had to wipe it down four or five times until it was finally clear enough for me to use … only I wish I had never cleared it."

For Nancy, who says she had never really considered herself to be the superstitious type or someone who believed in ghosts, the next part of the story is especially difficult for her to tell.

"But I swear to God that this really happened," she stresses.

Nancy explains that it's important to note that she lives alone and there was no one else in her apartment with her on this particular morning.

"That's important to understand because after I wiped the mirror clear and looked into it, what I saw scared the life out of me … when I looked into the mirror what I saw was a different person — a woman — looking back at me," she says.

It scared her so badly she says that she immediately broke down in tears. She also went immediately to the phone and called her mother because she had to tell someone what was happening in her apartment.

"Mom couldn't believe it either," Nancy says. "She was especially freaked out over what I told her next."

Despite never having met the woman who had died in the car accident, Nancy explains she had a clear image of what the young mother and wife looked like as her husband had showed her a picture of his wife when he came to the hospital to be with their son.

"There is no doubt in my mind that the face looking back at from the mirror was that of the woman who had died in the horrific car accident the previous night," Nancy says.

Was her mind playing tricks on her or was she so emotionally distraught over the accident that she imagined seeing the woman? She agrees that that is possible.

"But not likely," she says. "I know what I saw and I know for certain that when I looked into that mirror it wasn't me staring back at me. I'm one hundred per cent convinced that the woman looking back at me was the deceased woman."

The bigger question on Nancy's mind wasn't so much if it was the woman or not, but rather, why would the spirit of this deceased woman reach out to her and how would she know where to find her?

"I never had any contact with the woman," Nancy says. "She died at the scene, and if they brought her body to the hospital, I didn't see it, so I have no idea why she would reach out to me."

The only thing she can think of she says is that she may have been the last person to see the little boy alive just before he passed.

"I suppose it's possible that in some way, this woman tried to reach out to me because of my contact with her son," Nancy says. "But obviously, I just don't know."

She says despite being scared to death, in a way it's comforting to think that this mother, who would never be with her little boy again, was, perhaps, trying to find him.

"The image lasted only a few seconds and I'll admit that I was freaking out, but I remember that the woman seemed so sad and I remember that I instantly felt sad for her," Nancy says.

Whatever compelled this woman to reach out to Nancy will never be known, but her sudden appearance has convinced Nancy that there is more to life than we can imagine.

"Was this the woman's spirit or ghost?" Nancy wonders. "I've never been one to believe in such things, but I have to tell you that after seeing that woman's face in the mirror, I'm convinced that there's more to this life than could ever be known. Now, after all this, I'm just not so sure."

Gone With the Wind

He'll admit that it could have been the wind, but then he insists that he doesn't believe it was and, in fact, he believes it was actually something that defies a normal explanation.

It was the winter of 1971, Bill recalls, and he was staying at his grandparents' home near Antigonish. February 25, to be exact, he adds, pointing out that he will never forget that date for as long as he lives, because it was on that date that he was the most scared he's ever been in his entire life.

It was a stormy night, he begins, noting that it was snowing hard as the sun went down. The wind was blowing fiercely, he recalls, making it one of those nights where everyone was hunkered down in their homes and traffic on the roads consisted only of snowploughs and emergency vehicles, but then even those were only moving sporadically.

"I think what we had was a good ole nor'easter," he suggests.

At this point, it's worth pointing out that while Bill has agreed to tell his story, he will do so only if he can remain anonymous out of fear that others may question his credibility. He fears this because when he's told this story in the past he has been embarrassed and ridiculed.

"But," he says, "I assure you that what happened to me that night was not the stuff of fantasy or whimsy. I was 14 years old at the time and I know for certain what happened that snowy night because I can remember just like it happened yesterday and," he pauses and then continues, "it's not something I will ever forget. It freaked me out and left an indelible image on my memory that just won't go away, even after all of this time."

Bill, who was staying with his grandparents while his parents were away on two weeks' vacation, recalls that after he watched some television and finished up some homework, he went to bed around 11 o'clock.

"By that time the snow had all but stopped, but the wind was still blowing pretty hard, I remember that much," he says. "I also remember that I had difficulty falling to sleep that night because the wind was howling so loudly. It was whipping things around pretty good and causing the snow to bluster into major drifts. It wasn't a good night whatsoever; one of those nights to be inside, that's for sure."

Eventually, however, Bill says he somehow managed to dose off and it seems to him that he was having a great sleep until all of sudden, sometime just after 2 a.m. he was awoken by something hitting the bedroom window.

"Now when I stayed at my grandparents' house I slept in the same small bedroom that my father slept in when he was growing up," Bill explains. "It was a small room, down a narrow hallway that was just off the kitchen. My grandparents were sleeping in another room on the other side of the kitchen, so I knew that whatever it was that had awoken me, it wasn't them."

Bill says he just lay in the bed and tried to figure out what he had heard, but the longer he laid there, the more anxious he became.

"It was pitch black in the room and even though the wind had died down some, it was still blowing outside so as I laid there, I just kept telling myself over and over that it was the wind and that it had blown something up against the window."

Bill says he has no idea how long he laid there, maybe five or six minutes, but finally he heard the noise again and it scared him half to death.

"Just as sure as I'm sitting here talking to you today, I promise you that what I heard was three knocks on the window," Bill says. "It might have been the wind, but I know it wasn't because the pattern was too precise. It was three very distinct knocks, as if someone was outside the window."

He says he was paralysed with fear.

"I lay there in the dark and prayed that whatever was out there would just go away," he recalls. "I really didn't know what else to do. My heart was beating so fast and so strong, that I was afraid it was going to jump right out of my chest."

He says that the head of the bed was near the window so, as a mind will do under such circumstances, his mind raced with the possibilities.

"What if someone—or something—was outside my window? What if they got the window open? If that happened, they could reach in through the window and grab me," Bill says, recalling that he finally convinced himself that he should sit up in the bed. "Just to get away from the window," he chuckles nervously, the apprehension still evident after all these years.

"So that's what I did," he says. "I didn't know if I should move or not, but somehow I convinced myself to move and I sat up in the middle of the bed for a few minutes. Like I said, I just didn't know what to do. It was pitch black in the room and I couldn't see anything, so I just sat there and prayed that whatever was outside my window would just go away and leave me alone. I'll admit that I was terrified."

Bill says he has no idea how long he stayed there, just waiting for whatever was going to happen.

"What that was," he adds, "I have no idea. I don't really know what I was waiting for, but it seemed like I was sitting there for the longest while and then it happened again. Suddenly, I heard the knocks again. There were three very loud, very distinct knocks and I am certain that it wasn't the wind. I am absolutely positive about that. The pattern was too distinct for it to be the wind."

Bill says that he didn't hesitate this time. He knew his grandparents would be sleeping and they might be upset if he bothered them, but there was no way he was sticking around in that bedroom all by himself as he was certain that something was outside his window and whatever it was, it was trying to get inside ... trying to get him.

"My grandparents must have thought the house was burning down or something," he says. "The way I flew into their bedroom, it's a wonder I didn't scare them to death," he says.

He quickly told the elderly couple what happened and of course, Bill says, they immediately dismissed it as a bad dream or his imagination playing tricks on him in a bad storm.

"But they could see I was really terrified so they got out of their bed and went back to the room with me," Bill recalls. "Even though they were with me, I was still terrified. I was certain that something was out to get me. What it was or why it wanted me, I have no idea, but I can tell you it left me pretty shaken."

Following his grandparents back into the room, Bill says he dreaded the idea of having to go back to bed by himself.

"I just didn't like that idea at all," he says. "But it was late and I knew my grandparents would want me to go back to bed so I followed them and my grandfather went directly to the window and immediately opened the curtains. At that point, my imagination went into overdrive. I just had this vision that when my grandfather opened the curtains there would be some kind of hideous monster out there staring in at us ... but there wasn't."

He watched as his grandfather gave the window a good inspection and then promptly closed the curtains again.

"There was nothing there, he proclaimed and told me to go back to bed," Bill recalls. "He said I was too old for such foolishness, but that was my no-nonsense grandfather. There was no beating around the bush with him. He was pretty direct in everything he did. The light in the hallway helped a bit," Bill says, "but I never did go back to sleep that night. Instead, I laid there all night just waiting for the knocking to start again, but thankfully it never did."

Bill says that the next morning he couldn't wait to get out of that room, and after breakfast, with a great deal of reservation, he followed his grandfather around the back of the house to where the bedroom window was located.

"The snow was really deep and it was hard going but I guess he wanted to show me that there was nothing outside my window the night before," Bill says, "but to his surprise, he found more than he bargained for."

Bill recalls that just outside the bedroom window, they found a set of tracks or footprints in the deep snow, as if someone or something had been standing outside the window.

"My grandfather really didn't say too much," Bill says, "but I could tell he was spooked by what he saw. I could tell by the way he looked around the yard and visually followed the tracks to a growth of dense trees that lined the back of the property that he finally believed that something had, indeed, been there."

While Bill says they never determined what made the tracks, they were sure that it wasn't anything human.

"The prints looked animal to me," Bill recalls, "but the strange thing about them was that it looked like they were made by an animal walking on two legs, not four. That's the part that scared me."

Even after all these years, Bill admits that talking about the incident still gives him the creeps.

"I have no idea what was outside my window that night," he says, the fear still visible when he speaks of the incident. "And if my grandfather ever had any idea what it was, he never told me about it. In fact, we never talked about it much. Whenever I tried to bring up what happened that night, he'd quickly change the subject. He's gone now but the mystery remains and to this day I have no idea what was outside the window that night."

The Loyalist Ghosts

The Loyalist Inn is said to be one of the oldest properties in the Town of Shelburne. It's also said to be haunted.

Today, Shelburne is a small town located on the South Shore of Nova Scotia, but more than 200 years ago it was a hustling, bustling metropolis with thousands of residents.

Shelburne was settled on May 4, 1783, when 3,000 United Empire Loyalists, who had maintained allegiance to the British Crown (King George) during the American Revolution, arrived by ship from New York City. The Loyalists continued to arrive in large groups until 1784-85 when the population reached nearly 16,000.

As a result of this migration, Shelburne became the fourth largest community in North America in 1783. The population, which had grown so quickly, then decreased within 20 years to a few hundred, as the Loyalists moved on to other locations, but the town of Shelburne survived, although at a much smaller size.

Many descendants of the original Loyalists still live in the area. And, it seems, according to local legends, along with those living descendants are the spirits of those who refuse to leave or those who are unable to let go of their earthly existence. While famous for its Loyalist heritage, Shelburne is also a ghost enthusiast's dream. Multiple sightings have been reported throughout the community at numerous locations, and the townspeople are more than willing to share their stories with anyone who asks.

The Loyalist Inn in Shelburne is a particularly creepy place, with several ghost stories that have survived throughout the generations. The establishment boasts a couple of ghosts, one in the pub downstairs and the other in a guest room where paranormal phenomena has been reported for many years. The place oozes antique charm and creepiness … a ghost hunter's paradise.

Established in 1888, The Loyalist Inn has a long and colourful history in Shelburne. It may have been the original site of the Merchant's Coffee House where the first Loyalist founders gathered to discuss the daily happenings in what suddenly became the fourth largest city in North America.

For many years, The Loyalist Inn Hotel was known as the Bower Hotel and today, The Loyalist Inn Hotel is the last remaining hotel in Shelburne. It is perfectly located in the centre of the historic district where you can walk to Dock Street and just about everywhere else.

Gary, the current owner, tells stories of a ghost who has been seen and actually photographed sitting at the bar in the ground floor level tavern as if he's enjoying a beer.

"He's a quick fellow," Gary says. "One minute you see him and then next minute he's gone, so you have to be fast if you want to catch a glimpse of him. Most times, he's been there and gone before you even realize what you've seen. No one knows the identity of the spirit, but he's said to have been a part of the premises for many years. When you're back here behind the bar or out back working in the kitchen," he adds, "you can hear someone walking around on the floor and you can also hear some-one moving things around, but when you come to check things out, you quickly discover that there's no one here … except maybe the ghost and sometimes, even though there has never been any reason to be afraid of our visi-tor, it does make your skin crawl."

Another phenomena that he's observed in the bar and dining room areas of the inn is the unmistakable smells of dinner cooking in the oven, only there's nothing happening in the kitchen.

"The one thing I really notice," he says, "is the smell of turkey cooking." He chuckles, "There's no mistaking that odour. It smells exactly like someone cooking a full turkey dinner, even when there's no turkey on the menu."

Before buying the inn, Gary admits he had heard many of the supposed ghost stories about the existence of spirits that seemed to haunt the third floor of the build-ing and some of the guest rooms, but he never allowed those legends to influence his decision because he fig-ured that a certain amount of history would come with any building as old as The Loyalist Inn.

One of the more popular stories that have been passed down over the years is that The Loyalist Inn is home to a man who left the army and was promised a land grant for his service. The land never came. This was something that happened far too often to black loyalists at the turn of the last century and now, the story goes, the man is roaming the halls of the inn looking for some sort of recompense for the broken promise.

While many guests and employees of The Loyalist Inn have reported strange and unusual happenings throughout the historic property, one of the more "sensitive" employees to experience a "presence" is Elaine Stewart.

A native of Barrington, Shelburne County, Elaine has worked in the inn's housekeeping department for more than five years. She says almost from the first day when she began working there, she started to experience "strange" things happening no matter where she went in the building.

"For one thing, I'd go into a room and find that the lights were on even though no one was in the room," she explains. "I'd turn the lights off, leave the room and then go back in only to find that the lights had been turned back on. That was a little disturbing."

While she says she found that pretty weird, she tried to shrug it off and go about her business because it wasn't the first time in her life that she had experienced strange phenomena. She says she had grown accustomed to having unusual things happening around her.

"It started when I was a kid growing up in Barrington," Elaine says. "I just felt and saw things that other people couldn't and I guess I just kind of got used to it."

So she adds, while she encountered unusual happenings at The Loyalist Inn, she really didn't think much about it and over the years learned to take it in stride.

"I never felt afraid," she says. "I can't say I've felt threatened or intimidated by any of these things that happened around me. It has just become part of the everyday routine here at this place, but there are a few places where I don't feel comfortable. Like Room 9," she says. "I just don't like going into Room 9," Elaine explains. "It just doesn't feel right to me and I get a strange feeling whenever I go in there. For one thing, the air feels really heavy and when I'm in there working, the room door will close, even when I pry it open. It happens a lot."

To her knowledge, she says, nothing bad has happened in that room, but she knows the building is old with a long history and she insists that something is "off" about that room.

"For instance, after I go in there and make the bed, and then look at it, it's just like someone has been sitting on it," she says. "It looks like you can actually see the print where someone has sat on the bedspread. I've made a lot of beds over the years and I've never seen anything like that anywhere else. There's no explanation for that behaviour."

Another thing that Elaine says she doesn't like about some of the rooms in The Loyalist Inn is that she constantly has the feeling that someone is watching her even when she knows she's alone.

"You know how it feels when someone is watching you and you look around to see if anyone is around you?" she asks. "Well, that's how it is in some of the rooms here at the inn, only when you turn around there's never anyone there."

She adds that she can never shake the feeling that someone is watching her.

"They never show themselves," Elaine says. "And even though I never feel afraid of these things, I'm convinced that someone is there. But no, I have never been afraid in the place."

In addition to feeling as though she's being watched, she says, she has had other experiences at the inn that have convinced her that something ghostly exists there.

Like her boss, Elaine too has also experienced the unusual smells at the inn on many occasions.

"I've smelled turkey and bread baking and I've actually gone into the kitchen to see who was working, only when I got there, the place was empty and there was nothing in the oven," she says. "Both turkey and bread have very distinct smells when they're baking so I know what I've smelled. That has happened several times to me."

Additionally, Elaine says, there have been times when she has been up on the second floor working and she's heard her name being called from the main floor, only when she's come down to check out who was calling, her colleagues insist none of them had called her name.

"But I know what I heard," she says. "Someone was calling my name—Elaine—as clear as day. I heard it three times and each time, the others insist that they had not called me. … If it wasn't them, then who was it?"

While Elaine says most of her experiences at The Loyalist Inn have been sounds and smells, she admits to having one incident when she is certain she saw something out of the corner of her eye at the top of the stairs that lead from the main level to the guest rooms.

"It wasn't there long," she says. "Just the split of a second but I am certain that I saw something—maybe a man—at the top of the stairs. He was there and then he was gone. I have no idea who it was and none of the workers were anywhere close to the area so I just don't know."

While Elaine doesn't like to say she saw a ghost that day she does add, "I have only ever had this experience once but it gave me cold chills. It was there and then it was gone. Whatever it was, it wasn't natural."

Who or what roams the hallways and rooms of the historic Loyalist Inn remains a mystery but those who have spent time there, like Gary and Elaine, insist that whatever it is, it isn't from this world. But they also insist that whatever it is, it's of the benevolent persuasion.

The Haunting of Seminary House

A t the Seminary House, now a student residence at the historic Acadia University in Wolfville, it's not unusual to see lights turn on and off by themselves or to hear footsteps going up and down the back stairwell. Nor is it unusual to see doors open and close on their own, to observe objects move by themselves, or to hear disembodied voices throughout the residence.

Over the years, some guests and residents have also claimed to have seen a young, blond woman wandering about the rooms and hallways, opening and closing doors behind her as she goes. Those who have seen the young woman describe her as polite and demure. Those who believe in such paranormal activity also believe this restless spirit to be the ghost of an unfortunate unwed mother-to-be whose life came to a sad end at the Seminary House.

Located in the Annapolis Valley town of Wolfville, Acadia University was founded in 1838 as Queen's College, a preparatory university for future Baptist ministers. Renamed Acadia College in 1841, the first degrees were awarded in1843 and the first female graduate, Clara Belle Marshall, came in 1879.

In 1891, after being fully certified, the school switched names a final time to become Acadia University. Despite the Baptist Church continuing to hold nine of the board of governor's seats, Acadia has been non-denominational since 1966, and is recognized as one of Canada's top undergraduate universities.

In 1878, Acadia Ladies' Seminary was built as a companion to the men's college. Created as a finishing school for young, baptist ladies, Seminary House still stands today as the oldest building on the campus. For decades, it has served as a residence and, unlike in its early days, has been fully co-ed for years.

Seminary House is best descried as a lovely old place that, following renovations, is also now home to the School of Education and has been the residence of choice among those studying the fine arts. It draws in the sort of people who appreciate hand-carved wooden trim and the aura of heritage. It is also quite popular with the type of people who like a ghost in residence, and few are more enthusiastic about ghosts than the university arts crowd. So the question is, who haunts Seminary House? While her name has been lost with the passage of time, her story has survived and has been passed down year after year, so that it has become part of campus lore.

The story goes that in the late 1800s, shortly after Acadia Ladies' Seminary opened, one of the students housed there discovered that she was pregnant. For a well-to-do young lady of upstanding baptist roots, the Nova Scotia of the 1800s was no place to be an unwed mother. Unable to think of any better options, the girl hung herself, slipping into the open space between a banister and the back stairwell.

After the Ladies' Seminary closed, and female students were accepted into the general university population, Seminary House began its transformation into a full-time residence. At that time, reports began to trickle out of noises heard in what was called the Prophet's Room, which in actuality was a suite of chambers often let out to visiting lecturers.

The Prophet's Room is actually a small suite of rooms and was built with the residence in 1879. These are the oldest rooms on the campus and they are mainly used for visiting lecturers needing a place to stay. More than one guest claimed to have seen the pale spirit of a blond lady wandering the rooms, politely closing doors behind her as she passed.

One guest lecturer, who stayed in the room several years ago, reported that on the first night he was there, he suddenly awoke to find the windows open and a light wind blowing on the curtains, even though he was certain that he had closed the window before going to bed. When he looked around the room he noticed a young woman with blond hair sitting at the dresser combing her hair. She seemed to him to be semi-transparent and he shut his eyes and hid under the covers. For a bit, he heard pacing noises but then everything went quiet and all was gone when he looked out from under the covers.

That's the nice thing about the Seminary House ghost because, according to those who have encountered her over the years, she is not reported as a troublemaker. She keeps to her own space, limiting most of her nocturnal wandering to a television lounge, study area and, of course, the back staircase. Many students say they can hear her footsteps going up and down at night, and that if she passed you on your way to the basement laundry room, you would feel a cold chill and hear her quiet step, but no one feels threatened or intimidated by the young woman.

This Ghost Horses Around

The historic Fo'c'sle Tavern in Chester is said to be home to more than one apparition—one with two legs and one with four legs.

Photo by Vernon Oickle

What do you get when you take two men, a horse, an historical building and an argument that culminate in murder and mayhem? Well, at the famous Fo'c'sle Tavern in Chester you end up with a ghost story that's become the stuff of local legend.

Until the fall of 2014, The Fo'c'sle Tavern in Chester had the distinction of being known as the oldest rural pub in Nova Scotia, while the Seahorse Tavern in Halifax was known to be the oldest pub in the province. However, since the Seahorse moved from its former location in 2014 and required a new license, that ultimately made the Fo'c'sle the oldest drinking establishment in the province.

This record is simple to verify, as all pubs and taverns in Nova Scotia were prohibited by law to sell alcohol during the Prohibition Years, meaning modern records date back to 1946-47, which is when The Fo'c'sle received its liquor license.

But the building in which the modern tavern is located has a rich history. The Fo'c'sle has been in operation since 1764 in one form or another—not only as a tavern, but throughout the years some parts of the building were also used as an inn, a grocery store, and even as stables.

In fact, current owner Bob Youden, who purchased the property in June 2009 with his wife Audrey, points out that in the section of the pub where a pool table is currently located, it is possible to still see the original wood that was the framework for the stables, a feature that adds a certain character to the historic building. It is this section of the building that plays prominently into our story.

When the Youdens bought the building, Bob says they made a commitment to maintain its historic integrity, as it has been the focal point of the community for so many years. Furthermore, he points out, he and Audrey were not only looking to buy a business, but they also wanted to get involved in providing services for the community. Today, the establishment provides 19 year-round jobs and 24 seasonal jobs, also making it one of the area's largest employers.

"This place has been the hub of the village in one form or another for hundreds of years and it was our plan to keep it going that way," he says, adding that since they assumed ownership, they have undertaken some renovations to improve the building's infrastructure, but they have taken care to keep its character so that it continued to meet the community's needs.

"It has turned out to be everything that we had hoped it would be," Bob says, noting that since their daughter, Penny, joined the family business about two years ago as the pub manager, they have continued to experience great success.

Originally from Newfoundland, the Youdens moved to Chester almost ten years ago after Bob retired from a job in the United States, where they spent 20 years. When they decided to return to the Maritimes and started looking for a place to buy property they settled in Chester.

He says as their way of saying thank you to the community, every year, The Fo'c'sle has a New Year's Day levee and provides the food free of charge to the hundreds of people who attend. The Fo'c'sle also supports community events by providing the building for the Coldest Day of the Year, a benefit held every February to support the Chester Drama Society.

The Fo'c'sle is open 364 days a year, closing only on Christmas Day. It should come as a surprise to no one that a building with such historical significance comes with its own ghost or at least its own ghost story.

Yes, it's true and in fact, the Fo'c'sle comes not with one ghost, but two—one of a man and, of all things, one of a horse. The story goes way back, Bob points out, explaining that the events began sometime early in the 1800s, when the stables were still part of the business.

"It's said that the events began when two men were arguing in the tavern over the ownership of a horse that was being kept in the stables," Bob begins. "One of the men was staying in the boarding house upstairs while the other man was from the village."

What happened next really remains a mystery as the day following the argument, the horse was found dead in the stable and of course the men blamed each other for causing the animal's death, so the argument not only continued, but escalated.

"The night following the horse's death, the man who was staying at the boarding house was found dead in his room but," Bob explains, "while everyone suspected he was killed by the other man involved in the argument, no one was ever charged in connection with this crime."

Perhaps it was because no one was ever punished for his death, but in the years following the killing, stories began emerging that strange things were happening at the tavern and even today, Bob says, some of his staff report unusual activity at the Fo'c'sle such as cupboard doors opening and closing on their own, strange noises being heard in the area where the stable was located (now the location of the bar's pool table) and sometimes footsteps being heard on the second floor when there's no one up there.

In fact, he adds, although he has never personally experienced anything out of the ordinary at the tavern, some of his staff and some visitors have reported unusual things happening there.

"We have one woman who refuses to be in the place by herself so she won't open or close up for us," he says. "She doesn't talk about it much, but it's clear that whatever happened to her here left an impression so we work around her."

While many people attribute the strange occurrences at the Fo'c'sle to these incidents in history, no one can say for sure if that's the case, but Bob explains that they've invited paranormal investigators to the premises over the years and those efforts have confirmed a "spiritual" presence within the tavern, especially on the second floor.

Does Bob believe that a ghost or ghosts haunt his business?

Although he won't go quite that far, he does admit that he believes "something" happens there and whatever it is, he understands that it affects different people in different ways. But mostly, he adds, it's a fun piece of history that adds character to the building and it's part of folklore that makes the Fo'c'sle such a special place.

Ghosts at the Galley

The night of Monday, October 20, 2014 was clear and cold. The wind that had been blowing earlier in the day had died down and the mosquitoes of the summer were long since passed. It was a perfect night for a paranormal investigation.

It was 8 p.m. and eight intrepid members of the Crossed Over Paranormal Society (COPS)—Linda Rafuse, Kelly Connolly, Evan Rafuse, Lindsay Ingram, Brittany Wolfe, Stevie Hatt, Donna Doucette and Irene Hupman—arrived at the Galley Restaurant and Lounge in Marriott's Cove near Chester to conduct a paranormal investigation, their second at that location.

The group quickly formed three teams and went to various parts of the building to set up cameras and recording equipment, tools that are used to capture the images or sounds and voices from those who might occupy the space in another dimension. One team went to the basement where a lot of activity had previously occurred during the team's first visit to the location, a second group went to the kitchen area and the third group went to the lounge area. In all cases, the lights were turned out and people sat or stood quietly while the team leader spoke softly and respectfully, asking for responses to questions.

A paranormal investigation requires patience. After about an hour in those initial locations, the three teams regrouped to compare experiences to that point in the investigations. Not surprising to the members, two groups had definitely encountered unexplained activity. The next step was for the teams to swap locations so new ears and eyes could focus on the target areas. This continued until approximately midnight when the equipment was gathered and the team members headed for home. The recordings and pictures were all carefully scrutinized, dozens of hours of recordings and hundreds of photographs were dissected and studied, and then the findings were presented to the owners.

Ben Wiper, who owns the restaurant with his brother Jeff, explained the reasons for the investigations.

"There have been happenings that we can't explain; we thought we should ask someone to look into things. No one has ever felt threatened by anything that has happened here but we were hoping for answers," he says.

The brothers agree that while they know some people are skeptical about these encounters, they point out that they've both had experiences on the premises that cannot be easily explained or dismissed, so they remain convinced that something other than people inhabit the property.

Built in 1983, Ben says their experiences show that most of the activity at the Galley takes place from between 9:30 p.m. until 2 a.m. Originally owned by the Stevens family, the property was the site of a now demolished house and several outbuildings that were used for storage and workshops. While there isn't much known about the original owner, Ben says it appears as though a gentleman named John Stevens built the original house in the early 1800s.

"We haven't been able to find out much about Mr. Stevens, but we've been led to believe he was one of the area's original settlers," Ben explains. "We've also been told he worked as a brick mason and the story goes that he wasn't a very nice man. In fact, we've been told he supposedly was very abusive to his wife and children. Apparently, based on everything we've been told, Mr. Stevens was pretty rough with his family."

Although the Wipers have not been able to locate any proof or records to support this story, they point out that several years ago during a paranormal investigation, they heard some disturbing information that may, more or less, support this story.

"A medium who was on the site became very upset when she detected the spirit of woman who was suffering and in a great deal of pain," Ben explains. "She was very upset over what she was feeling. The medium indicated that she felt Stevens' wife had been trapped here, on the site, and couldn't get out. She was trapped somehow or confined against her will in a bricked up, enclosed space and couldn't get out."

The Wiper brothers point out that it is interesting to note that John Stevens was a mason so the brick part makes sense, and the corner of one of the old outbuildings was located directly where the entrance of the new building was constructed. Based upon what the medium told them, they believe that is the location where the woman appears to be trapped.

"Right from the beginning we knew there was something unnatural here," Ben says. "Shortly after we bought the building, Jeff, one other guy and I were in here painting one evening when a large ship's bell that hangs over the entrance door clanged for no reason. No one was near it and there was no wind and no doors were open so there's no way it could have rung on its own, but we all heard it. We're sure of that."

The brothers quickly add that the ringing ship's bell is not the only strange thing they've heard on the restaurant.

"We've had lots of strange goings on in the place," they agree.

For instance, they've heard people walking up and down the stairs only to realize there is no one there, and they've experienced the lights in the lounge going off and on even though there is no one in there. As well, it's fairly common for people working in the kitchen to see some-one walking past the windows in the kitchen doors, but when they go and check there is never anyone there.

"It's more than a little creepy," Jeff says. "When you're walking around in here at night you can hear and feel someone following you around. It makes you feel uneasy," he adds. "It really does give you the creeps, and one night, I even heard what I'm sure was the sound of a young girl trying to communicate with me. There was no mistaking that it was a young girl. I heard it as plain as day."

But the Wiper brothers are not the only ones who ex-perienced strange phenomena in the restaurant.

Jeff continues, "We've heard many stories of staff in the lounge who will be walking backwards as they're mopping up and then suddenly they will feel a hand on their backs, stopping them from going any further, but there is no one there."

However, they insist that it feels like someone has stopped them dead in their tracks and they say it feels like a hand touching them in the middle of their backs.

"It also happens with outsiders," Jeff points out. "When we were trying to get things ready to move in, we had a contractor in doing some work for us and he was up a ladder, working on the ceiling, but when he went to come down the ladder he felt a hand on his back and it was preventing him from going any further," he says.

While the Wipers say they don't believe whatever spirit is haunting their restaurant means to cause anyone harm, there are times when it seems like a dark cloud has moved in and a sense of foreboding settles over the place.

"Getting back to that earlier medium, she told us that she could sense that at some point in the past, a finger was removed from someone's hand, wrapped in a black handkerchief and then buried in the corner of the old building that had previously been located on the spot," Ben says.

Could that have had something to do with whatever is happening on the property? The brothers aren't sure, but the story certainly adds to the overall ambiance of the place.

"Based on everything we've heard and experienced, we think all of these happenings have something to do with the original owner of this property," Ben says. "We think that man is down there in the basement and when people go there they come up with such a negative feeling. There is definitely anger and depression down in the basement as well as prevalent feelings of sadness."

Despite all this paranormal activity and unexplained phenomena, the Wiper brothers have worked very hard to establish the Galley Restaurant and Lounge as a premier dining destination in Nova Scotia and they say the possible presence of a spirit or apparition adds a certain atmosphere. As for the members of the Crossed Over Paranormal Activity, the group's leader, Linda Rafuse, says their investigation uncovered a wealth of evidence that something extraordinary was going on at that location, enough evidence that prompts her to label the Galley as one of the hottest sports her group has visited.

"There is definitely something there," she says. "The spirit presence is very strong."

The Ghosts of Louisbourg

The morning mist over the Fortress of Louisbourg creates an atmosphere that's just right for the ghosts that are said to haunt the historic property in Cape Breton.

The Fortress of Louisbourg is the largest reconstruction project in North America.

Today, according to local legend, the apparitions of earlier settlers who died of smallpox, or those who lost their lives in battle while defending the settlement, haunt the massive structure.

Over the years, ghosts have been seen roaming the historic grounds, wandering through the buildings and passing through the many tunnels that are part of the massive complex.

"I never believed in ghosts. I always thought that such talk was a bunch of foolishness with people making things up or with over-active imaginations," one witness—a man—is quoted as saying. "That is until I saw a nurse in the unconstructed part of the fortress. At first, I thought she was part of the historical re-creations or something like that because she was wearing really old clothing, but when I asked about it, I was told activity at that part of the fort is kept low key and none of the costumed workers go there, but I saw her and I could tell she was a nurse just by the way she was dressed."

Later, this witness learned that according to legend, there have been on-going reports of a nurse walking the grounds by the old hospital and she appears to weeping as she walks.

"That sounds exactly just like what I saw," the man says. "Based upon the descriptions I had heard and comparing them to what I had seen, I now believe that is exactly what I saw. I was reluctant to believe it at first, but now I am convinced that I saw a ghost there even though others may only think that I was seeing things. Sometimes, though, seeing is believing."

The historical significance of the Fortress of Louisbourg is undeniable. The original settlement was founded in 1713 by the French and developed over several decades into a thriving center for fishing and trade. Fortified against the threat of British invasion during the turbulent time of empire building, Louisbourg was besieged twice, before finally being destroyed in the 1760s.

Following that invasion, the site lay untouched until well into modern times, when archaeologists began to reconstruct the fortress as it was in the 18th century. Today, thousands of visitors experience life in Louisbourg as it was during its heyday. There are more than a dozen buildings open to the public, including three authentic working 18th century restaurants.

Completing the experience, during the summer months, hundreds of re-enactors or "animators" of all ages, from wealthy merchants to poor soldiers, populate the streets of the restored fortress working, playing, and living life just as they would have in 1744. However, while these actors bring life to history, on more than one occasion, visitors have not only reported seeing the nurse apparition mentioned earlier, but several other ghosts.

The Fortress of Louisburg is said to be haunted by at least four ghosts.

In addition to the previously mentioned nurse, one of the most prominent ghosts at the fortress is that of a sea captain, who is said to be helpful in that he has stopped people from falling on the stairs and has been known to give directions throughout the property. Some people have reported being greeted by the crusty captain, while others have said they've passed him and then, just as quickly as he appeared, he disappeared again.

Additionally, over the years, a violent poltergeist has been reported to be haunting the premises, most notably at the bastion bakery where items have been moved and toppled over for no apparent reason, some of it machinery, weighing over 300 pounds. As well, there have been on-going reports of property being damaged with no credible cause or explanation being identified, and doors have been locked and unlocked even though no one was known to be on the property.

And finally, one of the most disturbing reports that has come from Louisbourg over the years is that of the ghost of a crying child that is accompanied by the sounds of gunshots and cannon fire and screams of men in battle.

"It's more than a little disturbing," the witness says. "There's no clear indication as to what's wrong with the child, but based on the way she's crying, you almost get the feeling that she's in a great deal of pain or she's suffering somehow. Are the crying and the gunfire connected?

No one knows for sure, but it is very upsetting to hear that."

It's often said that historic locations such as the Fortress of Louisbourg exude their own personalities, so it only stands to reason that the spirits of past inhabitants would dwell there. The question is — do you believe it?

The Lady in Blue

"**I** saw her once, you know," begins the witness who claims to have seen the famous Lady in Blue that is reputed to haunt the shores around the world famous Peggy's Cove, a tourist destination of great acclaim.

"I swear," the woman continues. "One minute, she was right there in front of me and then, pouf [she snaps her fingers to emphasize her point] she was gone the next. She just disappeared right in front of my eyes and I'll admit it left me shaken. I'm not a really big believer in ghosts and things like that, but I will admit that seeing this lady in blue really freaked me out."

It was a foggy night in late August many years ago, the woman recalls and she had driven down to Peggy's Cove by herself to check out the world-famous location that she had heard so much about, but had never visited even though she was born and raised in Nova Scotia. After parking the car and following the trails along the rocks, she says she spotted a woman standing, all by herself, on the edge of some rocks and then, 'in the blink of an eye', she was gone.

Pausing to gather her thoughts, the witness continues, "I'll admit it freaked me out at first because honestly, the first thought that ran through my mind was that some woman had either just been swept into the ocean by a rogue wave or had just jumped in. Either way, the woman was gone and I felt I had to do something because I thought I had just watched a woman fall to her death."

However, she says, when she started telling people about what she had seen and where she had seen it, people's reactions were not what she had expected they would be. In fact, they were nonchalant about the whole thing, she recalls.

"Oh that?" they replied. "That's The Lady in Blue. She's seen around Peggy's Cove all the time, they told me. She's not in any danger because she's a ghost."

The witness says she was taken aback by the reaction, because what if it weren't this mysterious lady in blue? Were people just going to stand by and let the woman be drowned?

But in time, she says she eventually came to accept the truth—that she had a seen a ghost—whether she was willing to admit it or not.

Recalling the incident, she points out that what she had seen only lasted a few seconds, but she is convinced she saw a woman on the rocks.

"I know what I saw," she insists. "It only lasted a few seconds, but there absolutely was a woman there on the rocks and then she was gone. I'm positive about that. Was it a ghost?" she asks. "Well, it was something because when it happened I got goose bumps all over and the little hairs on my arms stood at attention. It gave me the willies and I got these strange sensations in the pit of my stomach, unlike anything I had ever experienced before. It left me pretty shaken. … In fact, it bothers me even to this day after all of this time."

The legend of The Lady in Blue that haunts the world famous Peggy's Cove has been passed down from one generation to the next for many decades. In fact, the location has been listed as one of the Top 10 Haunted Places in Canada, a point that further supports this witness's story, as she knows she is not alone in her experiences.

Nova Scotia is home to over 160 historic lighthouses and these majestic beacons can be found throughout the province. One of Nova Scotia's most well-known lighthouses and maybe the most photographed in Canada is Peggy's Point Lighthouse, known to many as Peggy's Cove Lighthouse. Located in the quaint fishing village of Peggy's Cove along the South Shore, Peggy's Point Lighthouse was built in 1915.

The image of this famous lighthouse on top of the giant rocks with the sea waves crashing in is just as beautiful today as it has been for almost a century. Peggy's Cove is famed for its picturesque and typically East-Coast profile, with houses perched along a narrow inlet and on wave-washed boulders facing the Atlantic. Although this unique environment has been designated a preservation area, it is still an active fishing community ... but as we've learned above, it's also famous for its ghost story. However, what's the story behind the world-famous legend?

In his book, This is Peggy's Cove, Bill deGarthe wrote: Many have asked, "How did Peggy's Cove get its name?"

There are two versions in existence and the first has more generally been accepted, because of its romantic and dramatic appeal to most people. The story goes that a schooner was wrecked on "Halibut Rock" off the Lighthouse Point, in a Southeaster, in sleet and fog on a dark October night. The ship ran hard aground and with high waves washing her decks, some of her crew climbed to the masts, but the waves washed them into the boiling sea. Everyone on board was lost except a woman, who managed to survive the turbulent seas, swam ashore and was finally rescued by the people on the shore.

Her name was Margaret, and she married one of the eligible bachelors of the Cove. The people from near-by places used to come and visit Peggy of the Cove, and before long they began to call the place Peggy's Cove. How true this story is, no one knows, and there are no documents available to confirm or refute it.

In the second version, perhaps not so romantic, but more logical, Peggy's Cove, being situated at the entrance to St. Margaret's Bay, was shortened from Margaret's Cove, to the more intimate name of Peggy's Cove, a name world famous now for a place of scenic beauty, where tourists gather from far and near.

But while either of these stories may, in fact, provide a reasonable explanation of how the name came about, there is actually a third tale that has a more worldly connection and may, in fact, provide some explanation to the origin of The Lady in Blue.

Local legend tells of a woman who resided on the land prior to the construction of the lighthouse. The story goes that she survived a shipwreck only to mourn her children lost to the sea. She would later lose her new husband in a tragic fall from the rocks of Peggy's Point. The fall was fatal. So devastated by her loss, it is said the woman went out for a walk one day on the very same rocks that claimed her husband's life and was never seen alive again.

Over the years, many people have seen her transparent figure in a blue dress standing on the rocks that claimed her husband, with her arms spread as if she is getting ready to jump. As soon as they run in an attempt to save her, she disappears from sight.

Is she bound to the earth because she took her own life? Perhaps, but you be the judge.

These photos, taken the day after a massive fire razed White Point Beach
Resort in November 2011, not only show the destruction
of the building but a closer look at the top window to the right may
also reveal something else. Take a close look. Is that the mysterious
Ivy that was reputed to haunt the property for many years?

Whatever Became of Ivy?

When the historic White Point Beach Resort, one of Nova Scotia's premier resort getaways located on the province's picturesque South Shore, was destroyed by fire in November 2011, the flames not only claimed the wooden structure and much of its priceless contents, but they may have also consumed Ivy, the property's resident ghost.

For years, it was said that the ghost of Ivy, who ran the dining room in the 1920s, roamed the main lodge, but after the massive fire, reported sightings of the ghost at the new lodge that opened one year following the disaster, have been slim to none. At the same time, however, reports of paranormal activity throughout some of the other resort facilities have increased leading some to speculate that, in fact, Ivy didn't perish in the fire, as originally thought, but instead, may have moved elsewhere on the premises where she roams freely around the property.

Ivy was the first wife of Howard Elliot, one of the original owners of White Point Beach Resort. She managed the resort's food and beverage department, maintaining very high standards for dining room staff. Perhaps a product of her time era, employees who worked there claimed that Ivy ran a very tight ship. In fact, it was said to be her way or the highway when it came to working in the kitchen and dining room.

Even after Ivy passed away, she was reluctant to give up control of the dining room. Over time, stories of Ivy's haunting ran the gamut of paranormal activity and included such happenings as spoons and ladles falling off the hooks in the kitchen of the original lodge. The real mystery here was that the hooks were an "S" shape, so things had to jump off them, not fall, and the laws of physics dictate that such things just don't happen.

Additionally, in the former lodge, many of the staff related stories of hearing their name being called during pre-meal set up, when they were alone and particularly after they had done something wrong. One former employee at White Point Beach Resort recalled her experiences with Ivy.

"Many times late in the evening, I'd be sitting in my office, located in the corner of the former dining room, and I would hear footsteps coming from the front of the dining room toward the kitchen. The door of the office was usually open, yet no one would ever appear. I always believed it was Ivy either checking to make sure I was working or wanting the office for herself. As I've said many times, even after her passing, she was reluctant to give up control."

The employee recounts another incident in which she encountered Ivy.

"One evening, I went downstairs for something—I can't remember exactly what it was. There were so many reasons to go down there. Once there, I saw a woman out of the corner of my eye in a flowing white pantsuit type of outfit. She was passing from the kitchen stairs through to the old games room. I really didn't think much of it because I had noticed another woman wearing a similar

120

outfit when she came to dinner earlier that evening, but when I went back upstairs, the other woman was still in her seat. When I asked the staff if she'd been away from the table, I was told no, and truthfully, when I thought of it, I wondered why the woman would be poking around in the basement in the first place when her husband and another couple were in the dining room having dinner?"

The more this employee thought about what she saw, the more she became convinced she had seen Ivy in the basement.

Another former employee tells a story of him and another crewmember coming to the lodge one winter day to plough the roads to the resort. This was before White Point was open year-round as it is today. As the two men came past the rose bush that used to be in the middle of the driveway at the front of the former main lodge, they watched as the front door opened and closed, although they hadn't seen anyone in the vicinity.

Not sure why the door would be unlocked, but thinking that the wind must have blown it opened and closed, the two men parked the truck and got out to investigate what they had just seen. When they did, they became alarmed when they noticed footprints in the snow leading to the front door. Inside, on the floor, they discovered droppings of snow as if it had fallen off someone's feet. Their first thought was that someone had broken in to the main building. The two men searched inside and outside the lodge, but no one could be found. As far as they knew, they were the only people on the property that cold winter day.

But Ivy may not be the only ghost that haunts the grounds of White Point Beach Resort, as it is said that the spirit of a former caretaker has also been reported over the years.

One former employee explains, "Many people believe the ghost of an older gentleman named Danny roams White Point. He was the caretaker here in the wintertime and the chef in the summer. He stayed in cabin 20. Today, it's unit 137. I worked with him between 1978 and 1979, and he was a great guy. I considered him a really good friend. Danny worked at White Point for a long time, and everyone said he was really good friends with Ivy. Apparently he worked for her when she lived in Halifax. He looked after the property for many years."

After Ivy died, many people reported seeing Danny roaming around the property, talking to someone who was never there.

"I saw it myself on many occasions," the former employee says. "When you'd go to his cabin, it was common to see him sitting by the table having a drink and having a great conversation with someone else, only there was never anyone else around. Whenever you asked him who he was talking to, he'd say Ivy was in and they were having a talk."

The cabin has been the site of many reported paranormal experiences over the years.

"We would get a lot of reports of lights going on and off in there, and the bed would sometimes be opened up, as if waiting for an occupant," the former employee says. "We just figured Danny was in there playing tricks. Different people reported seeing things in that cabin that they couldn't explain."

But Danny's haunting behaviour was not only confined to the cabin. There had been reports of people seeing a man and woman come out of the fog down on the beach and then suddenly disappear. Based upon the description of those who had seen the man and woman, many people believe the man was Danny, the former caretaker, while the woman was Ivy, the former owner's wife, and they had been out inspecting the premises as they often did.

As for Ivy, this employee says, he has heard many stories of her presence at the former lodge, but his own encounters with her made him a believer.

"There was a time when I didn't believe in that stuff, but I certainly do now following some of my experiences. The first one occurred around the year 2000 after a major snowstorm. We had been ploughing all day, trying to keep the roads clear. That night, one of the other guys and I were salting the walkways. When I got to room 55, I noticed a woman come around the corner of the building and walk toward where I was standing. I remember thinking that it was strange that she was wearing only a thin black coat, even though it was February with the wind blowing off the Atlantic."

He remembers it was pretty cold.

"As the woman got closer, I remember saying something like, 'Awful cold to be out tonight,' and she kept on going. At first I didn't pay it much attention, but as I kept on cleaning and salting the walkways, it suddenly hit me. Even though it had been snowing, the woman wasn't leaving behind any footprints. I followed her and when I was about six feet away, she just disappeared. I remember she was a tall, thin woman with long, brownish, coloured hair. I couldn't see her face, but I'm convinced it was Ivy. I couldn't tell if she was an older woman or young. Some people have seen her in her earlier years, but others have seen her as she was when she got older."

The second time he encountered Ivy happened in winter 2005–06.

"They called me from the front desk with a report that the heat in room 206 wasn't working, and they needed it turned on. I went to the room by way of the back stairs, which went to the upper level of the old lodge from the kitchen," he says. "It was the way staff travelled. On the way back down, I heard the heavy security door at the top of the stairs open and close. At first I thought it was a guest, but we don't allow the guests to travel that way. Then I saw a figure. I couldn't tell if it was a man or woman, but it was moving quickly and it was coming toward me. It went past me and went into the kitchen. I don't know what it was but it was something. I could feel it as it went by, and it was cold," he says.

He points out that when Ivy was alive and working at the old lodge, she always travelled down that particular stairwell to get to the kitchen.

Reports connected to Ivy had been a regular occurrence over the years in the old lodge.

"I remember one day when I was working from 11:00 at night to 7:00 in the morning. There were two guests staying in room 212, which was Ivy's room when she was at the lodge," he says. "The guests called the front desk around 5:00 a.m. to report that their bathroom light kept coming on even though the switch was turned off."

Checking out the bathroom, he determined there was nothing wrong with the electricity. The switch was in good working order, he says, adding that the male guest also reported that when he went to bed, rolled over and looked into the bathroom, he could see the picture of a woman hanging where the bathroom mirror was supposed to be—but there was never any such picture hanging there. He said the woman in the picture had long hair with flowers in it. She was a nice-looking woman, he observed. That sounded a lot like Ivy.

Another time, a guest staying in the same room came down for breakfast. She told one of the servers that she had been frightened through the night when she woke up and saw a woman standing beside her bed. She described the woman as being very thin, with flowers in her long hair. It was said that Ivy loved flowers and that she wore them in her hair a lot.

"There was also the time a woman, who was staying in what was Ivy's former room, woke up and saw a silhouette of a woman in the mirror. It frightened her so badly that she left and never went back there," he says. "Another time, at night, two of the girls who work in the Recreation Department walked past the old dining room on their way to the main desk to turn in their keys like they have to do every night. At one of the tables by the windows overlooking the shoreline, was a woman sitting, staring out at the waves. They knew the dining room was closed, but they thought one of the guests was sitting there enjoying the scenery. When they looked the second time, the woman was gone. They later learned that the location was Ivy's favourite table, and she would often come there and sit at night to watch the waves breaking on the shore just outside the dining room window."

There were many reports of unusual activity over the years at the old resort. Candles kept lighting on their own and wouldn't go out. There were reports of music playing in some rooms, even though the radios and televisions had not only been turned off, but also unplugged. Everyone who had worked at the front desk had heard footsteps going through the dining room late at night, and one morning, one of the clerks said she could hear wine glasses tinkling together even though the dining room was completely empty. It was spooky, there was no question about that.

However, when the fire of 2011 tore through the former lodge building, all of these stories and memories of Ivy went up in smoke and flames—or did they?

Following the disaster, reports began circulating of photos taken before and during the fire that clearly showed a woman standing in the building's windows. Was that Ivy? Was she watching as her beloved lodge was reduced to a pile of ash and smoldering embers?

Some think it was.

In the years following the opening of the new lodge, reports of paranormal activity have been almost nonexistent, but some believers think that Ivy's spirit still occupies the premises, and while she has kept a low profile in the new facilities, they believe she is still there looking over the place. They're just waiting for her to make her appearance.

The Bilingual Ghost

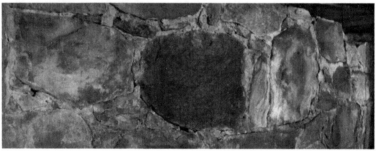

Dexter's Tavern, in the historic privateer town of Liverpool, is said to have several ghosts including a French solider. In the second photo, are the huge, squared stones of the foundation that may have come from the ruins of the Fortress Louisbourg.

When things go bump in the middle of the night at the historic property in Liverpool known as Dexter's Tavern, it's time to sit up and take notice because, based upon past anecdotal evidence, you just might have a visitor from another place—or perhaps even one from one another dimension.

For generations, residents of Liverpool and visitors to the privateering town have heard stories of a ghost that roams the halls and rooms of Dexter's Tavern, as well as the exterior perimeter of the property. It is said that this 1763 structure is haunted by a benevolent spirit dressed in a French soldier's uniform that spends most of its time walking back and forth on the floor of the master bedroom. However, over the years, some have also reported seeing the ghost of a small child roaming the property, but by far, the spirit of a French soldier is the most common sighting.

Although the bilingual ghost, as he has been labeled, is friendly most of the time, on occasion, he can also be mischievous, moving objects about and opening locked doors and windows. While most of the reports make him seem harmless enough, there have been times when the paranormal activity has been less than cordial. But why is the spirit of a French soldier haunting a property in a town that was settled by the English?

Well, that's a good question and one that previous owners and inhabitants have tried to answer for many years. While there is no concrete answer to that mystery, there is a widely accepted theory and several clues to support it.

Located in an historic district of Liverpool known as Fort Point, the tavern derives its name from original owners Enoch Dexter, a blacksmith in the early port settlement, and his wife, Mary. It was constructed from timber largely cut on the spot, while it is believed the huge squared stones of the foundation may have come from the ruins of the Fortress Louisbourg, a French fortification located in Cape Breton, as they were brought to Liverpool by cargo ships using them as ballast and then left there.

If one believes that spirits can become attached to inanimate objects, as a popular theory suggests, then it is entirely possible that this would explain how a French soldier was transported to an English port. Throughout the years, witnesses have reported seeing such a specter roaming the property on which Dexter's Tavern sits at the mouth of Liverpool Harbour, where the ships would have sailed.

Taverns during this time period were usually private homes that were open to the public, with the owners licensed to provide liquor, food and lodging, as was the case with the Dexter property. Taverns also served as auction rooms, assembly rooms, banqueting halls and general centres of entertainment. The first floor of the Dexter structure has two rooms—the "keeping room", where common people gathered for their drinks, and a dining room. It is not clear today, but there may have been a partition between the two that would have folded back for dances or large gatherings. The second floor had two bedchambers, called "boarding rooms" and they contained rows of bunks.

The American Revolution brought a garrison to the fort in Liverpool, located a stone's throw from Dexter's Tavern, as well as many Royal Navy ships loaded with sailors seeking marauding privateers. All of these soldiers and sailors likely visited the bar in search of libations. When her husband died in 1777, Mary Dexter carried on the business. After her death, the premises were used as a private dwelling and continue as such to this day. It has three floors with only two rooms on each floor. The storm porch is a later addition.

There is no recorded date as to when the ghost of Dexter's Tavern began to present itself, but the haunting has now become a staple of local folklore and legend, with homeowners, occupants and visitors reporting paranormal activity at varying degrees down through the decades. Also throughout the years, the severity of the haunting has fluctuated with witnesses reporting a variety of activity from a fleeting image in the corner of an eye to a full-on view of the ghostly soldier as he patrolled the fort tavern.

The types of shenanigans pulled by the ghost have also varied over the years, with witnesses reporting a range of feelings from curiosity and bewilderment to fear and anxiety while in the house. While some witnesses have felt acceptance for and by the spirit, others have felt so intimidated that they've left the premises, never to return.

Current owners, Bob and Jacquie Pearson, who purchased the historic property and moved to Liverpool from Calgary in September 2013, readily admit that they were fully aware that Dexter's Tavern allegedly came with a ghost, but they didn't allow the legends to dissuade them from making the decision to move there. When they found the place, while searching on line, they knew right away it was going to be their retirement home and they say they've enjoyed every minute they've spent there.

While they say they've heard many stories about the ghost or ghosts that supposedly roam the halls and rooms of their home, they have never felt intimated or afraid in the place. However, they do admit that sometimes the home does give off a strange "feeling" or vibe, but they credit that to the building's age and the years of history that have unfolded within its walls, not necessarily a ghost. Considering its age and the number of people who have passed through the doors over the centuries, the couple says they aren't surprised that the house would have some stories to tell.

Although the Pearsons have undertaken an extensive renovation of the property, they have remained committed to maintaining the historical and structural integrity of the building, but they have felt comfortable in their home from day one. During the renovations, Bob even discovered the large square stones in the basement that supposedly came from Fortress Louisbourg, but he has never experienced any type of paranormal activity while working around them.

However, both he and Jacquie are quick to point out that even though they themselves have never experienced the types of hauntings that some say they have encountered at Dexter's Tavern, they would never discount what others have reported experiencing. They accept that everyone's experiences would be different because people are not equally sensitive to such things. One such individual who wishes to remain anonymous and who lived in Dexter's Tavern before the Pearsons purchased the property, relates an entirely different experience in the house, one that involves frightening encounters with a malevolent spirit, which eventually forced her and her family to vacate the premises.

"I am convinced that there is something evil in that house," the woman insists, while talking about her time in Dexter's Tavern, which lasted almost two years. "What my family and I experienced when we lived there isn't natural and it can't be easily explained."

Almost from the time her family moved in, she immediately developed the feeling that someone—or something—was watching her.

"It didn't really matter where I went in the house, upstairs or downstairs, the kitchen or living room or the bedrooms, it felt like I was being watched, and I will admit that it made me feel uneasy," she recalls.

131

She quickly points out that she kept her thoughts to herself for fear of scaring her children, but eventually, she points out, that all changed because the children finally became so afraid that they did not want to be alone in the house.

"It was especially bad when they had to go upstairs where the bedrooms and bathroom are located," she explains. "It got so bad that either my husband or I had to go up with them because they just would not go upstairs on their own. They were that scared."

"In time," the woman says, "it got to the point that things began to go missing and they'd stay lost for days at a time—sometimes even weeks—only to turn up in places they had thoroughly searched. This would drive us crazy," she says. "We'd look and look and look, but could never find whatever it was, only the next day you'd find it right there in the exact spot where you had looked so many times before. It was more than a little creepy. Wallets were among the most popular of the missing items, but other things such as hairbrushes and keys also went missing."

In addition, the family reported that they all heard things moving about and they all heard the sounds of people walking, especially going up and down the stairs. She also reported that at times, the blankets on the bed in what was being used as the master bedroom would not stay up, as if someone were pulling them down. Furthermore, most of the family reported hearing and seeing doors opening and closing on their own, especially the closet in the master bedroom, and the baby constantly fussing whenever he went in the nursery.

"It was almost like someone was bothering him," she says. "When I went into the room that they used as a nursery, the baby would be standing up in the crib and crying. "It just didn't feel normal."

However, the worst incident happened one Christmas Eve several years ago when her husband was away for work.

"It was after midnight," she begins. "I had just gotten the kids settled down for the night and I was getting into bed myself when, all of a sudden, I heard the closet door squeak open. I quickly sat up and said, 'No. Not tonight. I am not doing this tonight so leave me alone', and the closet door closed again. I swear to God the door went closed and there is no possible way that could happen without a major wind blowing through the house and obviously there was no wind, so what could it have been?"

Several minutes later, just as she was getting settled again, she says she heard the baby starting to fuss and cry in the room that's located next to the master room. As she started to pull herself up, she immediately realized she could not push the covers down and she could not move. She felt trapped.

"It was like someone was sitting on my chest and pressing their knees into each of my shoulders, preventing me from getting up," she recalls. "I was literally pinned down on the bed with the blankets pulled up to my chin and there was no way I could get up. I was in a panic because I could hear the baby crying, so I started calling for my oldest son who was in a room down the hallway, but by the time he got to my room, whatever was on me and holding me down, had gone and I was sitting on the edge of the bed."

She pauses and then continues.

"But I will admit, it freaked me out. By the time I got to the baby's room he was standing and crying in his crib, but there was nothing else around," she says. "Whatever it was that had me pinned down in my bed, there was no way that I was getting up to go to him. It was pretty frightening, there's no doubt about that."

While the family did report having many encounters with the spirit and they all admit to being frightened at times, she points out that she does not ever think they felt threatened in any way.

"It was a little unnerving at times, I will admit," she says, "but I don't think the ghost ever meant to do us harm, or we never felt that at least."

Regardless, she adds they were glad and relieved when the time came to move out.

As for Bob and Jacquie Pearson, they admit they've heard these types of stories in the past, but have never had any such experiences of their own and they feel perfectly comfortable in their home.

"It's just all part of the bigger mystery," they agree. "And part of the house's character."

The Vampire of Ingonish

Located on the northeastern coast of Cape Breton Island, in the Village of Ingonish, is a world-class resort called the Keltic Lodge.

The land where the Keltic Lodge is situated was expropriated by the Nova Scotia government from Henry and Julia Corson of Akron, Ohio in 1936. The Middlehead Peninsula, on which the Corson's land was situated, was highly desired after the federal government created the Cape Breton Highlands National Park.

The Keltic Lodge was in operation for two seasons, but because of wartime shortages and overseas fighting, the government closed the hotel in 1942. In 1946, after the end of the war, the hotel reopened. In November 1997, an electrical fire claimed the gift shop and coffee complex sections of the resort. The blaze erupted on a stormy evening and local firefighters had to battle high winds and snow to save the nearby structures from harm. In 1999, the Atlantic Restaurant and Birch Tree Shop opened on the site of the original complex.

The Keltic Lodge continues to play a major role in the community of Ingonish, as a source of employment and as a major attraction, drawing tourists to the area. The mystique of the Keltic Lodge is enhanced by its prime location on the famous Cabot Trail, within Cape

Breton Highlands National Park, and by its proximity to Highlands Links, the number one golf course in Canada.

While the Keltic Lodge in itself has a rich and vibrant history reaching back for decades, what may not be so well known is that the facility also has a diverse and varied history of paranormal activity. This is one such story.

Doug Mombourquette has lived in Cape Breton his entire life and grew up in the shipyard area of Sydney. He's married and has two children, one 18 years old and one five years old. He studied Hospitality Administration at Cape Breton University, which is how he ended up working at the Keltic Lodge, and he explains that it was on a work term there, that he had his experience with the world of paranormal activity. He notes that his experiences at the Keltic Lodge were so profound that they got him interested in paranormal research.

Pointing out that this experience happened back in 1996 when he worked at the Keltic Lodge, he explains, "Based on my own personal experiences and the experiences of others in this field, I believe there has to be something more for us after we die."

In the summer of that year, Doug recalls, staff at the Keltic, as well as residents throughout the local community, reported that they had seen a strange man lurking around the area.

"The best way that I can describe him is that he was about six feet tall, possibly in his late 40s, and was wearing an older style, black tux, a long, flowing, black cape with red satin on the inside, a tall, wide-brim top hat and a very bright gold pocket watch. He was carrying a black walking stick with a gold ball on the top," he says.

What made this so strange, Doug points out was that he was only ever spotted after midnight.

"The first time I saw him I was moose spotting with one of my friends," he recalls. "I remember that when we passed the graveyard we noticed that there was a mist that seemed to rolling out across the street and this man was standing in the middle of it. It scared the hell out of us because this was around 2 a.m. and I didn't think there would be anyone else around at that hour."

What this man was doing dressed in such a fashion and roaming the streets at that time of day was not known to Doug and friend, but he says, "We dubbed him, The Vampire of Ingonish."

Following the incident, Doug says neither he nor his friend ever said anything to anyone about what they had seen because, he admits, they weren't exactly sure what they witnessed.

"We just chalked it up to us seeing things," he says. "About two weeks later, my girlfriend, who is now my wife, came back to Ingonish from a Sydney run with her friend. They came straight down to my room in residence and told me that they had just seen this man walking on the road towards the Keltic and described him perfectly."

Doug says her description was just like what he and his friend had seen, and he admits it freaked him out.

"At this point, my friend and I realized that this man must be for real but before this, we had just chalked it up to some local man walking around in the wee hours of the morning who likes to dress up," he says, "but here is where its gets weird."

"In 1996," he explains, "Ingonish was hit by storm surge and extremely high winds from a hurricane that was churning up the Atlantic. The night of the storm my girlfriend and I went out behind the White Birch Inn to watch the waves," Doug recalls. "The huge waves were crashing so hard along the cliffs that you could stick your arm over the safety railing and it would get wet."

He says that it was a major storm, and to this day, he does not remember ever again seeing waves that big.

"After being there for about ten minutes, my wife drew my attention to a patch of cliff further up the road from where we were standing and towards the main building," he says. "Standing half way down the cliff on a small little ledge was this man that we had seen before and he was all dressed up just like he was before. The ledge was so small that we didn't know how it was holding him and there is no way he could have got to that ledge without falling into the water below. He would have had to repel down the face of the cliff with ropes, and there were no ropes around. We just don't know he did it, especially in the middle of such a major storm."

Doug continues, "I'll swear this before a judge. The wind was not even causing his cape to stir, nor was he affected by the surf. The wave would crash in and it wouldn't even budge him. I started to scream to him to see if he needed any help, but he looked towards my wife and me and just nodded and smiled at us. Then, as the next wave was about to crash into him, he just vanished. It wasn't normal," he insists. "It was like the man just turned to vapor and left with the wave," he said. "I can still remember that night like it was yesterday."

And to this day, Doug says he has never been able to find a reasonable explanation of who this gentleman may have been or where he may have come from. However, he notes he has never seen him again and to his knowledge, neither has anyone else.

"And this is a small community," he says. "There's no way that he wouldn't be someone after all these years … no way."

The Blue Nun of St. Francis Xavier University

"**I** swear to God, someone was in my room," the university student says, chuckling at her choice of words since she was actually talking about the spirit of a nun that supposedly haunts one of Nova Scotia's finest universities, and one that has a strong historic connection to the Roman Catholic Church.

"I could sense its presence when I woke up," the student says. "It was like it was just standing in the center of the room, watching me while I was sleeping and then it was gone in an instant. I have no idea who it was, but I'm positive I wasn't alone."

Reports of hauntings at St. Francis Xavier University in Antigonish have become the stuff of legend. Throughout the years, students have seen apparitions of a nun in the games room, elevators moving with no occupants inside, ghostly figures that watch you climb stairs and even the sounds of footsteps, when no one is walking in the hallways.

But is the nun real or just wild stories invented by a wild and over-active imagination?

Students moving into St. Francis Xavier University's Mount St. Bernard residence, which has been named the

"Bear Cave" due to its underground passageways, soon learn that they have a ghostly dorm-mate—the Blue Nun.

This spectral sister has been known to knock over books, wash dishes, and startle students on the spiral staircase in Gilmora Hall. But who is this ghost? To answer that question, a little history lesson is needed.

Canada's St. Francis Xavier University, often called St. FX, was originally founded in 1853 as Arichat College, taking its name from the Nova Scotia town where it was located. In 1853, the Catholic university moved about 65 miles east to Antigonish and its name was changed.

In 1883, the Sisters of Notre Dame opened Mount St. Bernard Academy, a Catholic girls' school serving grades 1 to 12. The school changed its name to Mount St. Bernard College in 1890, transitioned to a women's college, and became affiliated with St. FX in 1894, graduating its first Bachelor of Arts students in 1897. By the 1920s, the schools were effectively merged, with both male and female students attending classes at Mount St. Bernard.

In 1937, the Gilmora Hall residence was built, and, over the years, the college was increasingly used as a dormitory. In 2001, St. FX purchased the college from the Sisters of Notre Dame. Today, it typically houses first and second year students, although both the nursing and jazz studies programs have facilities in Gilmora Hall.

According to legend, the Blue Nun was a member of the Sisters of Notre Dame, who fell in love with a priest and became riddled with guilt over the affair. Eventually, she was so overcome by despair, that she leapt to her death from a balcony in Gilmora Hall.

There are a few different versions of the story, but they all have the same general idea. Another version of the legend suggests the nun became pregnant and threw herself off the Gilmora balcony out of shame. It is said that the priest, overcome with grief, also later hung himself within the building.

Other versions of the story claim that the nun was sexually assaulted and jumped from the balcony, or that the priest pushed her and hung himself out of guilt. No matter what the origins, the supposed results are more or less consistent. Former residents of the Mount say that the nun, affectionately referred to as "the Blue Nun" still haunts the building.

The story goes that since her death, she has lingered on the property. In one version of the story, her beloved priest later hung himself and now also joins her in haunting the college.

While there are no records that any such a tragedy actually occurred at Mount St. Bernard, that should not be a big surprise as a ghost in a convent will generally be presumed to be a nun in love. In this case, most of the reports deal with phenomena, rather than sightings of a clear apparition, raising the question, why is the ghost called "blue."

There are many accounts from those who claim to have encountered the Blue Nun over the years.

For instance, in 2010, students attending a residence hall meeting were interrupted by what sounded like an antique phone ringing. A resident followed the sound to a second-floor payphone, but the ringing had stopped. Subsequent investigation found that the only public phone capable of receiving incoming calls was on the third floor, and that phone's ringer did not match what the students had heard.

Misbehaving electronics are apparently a recurring theme with the ghost. Students report lights and appliances turning on in the middle of the night, including a television that had been unplugged. Other phenomena include objects moving around on their own, such as textbooks and pushpins being strewn across dorm room floors. Doors slamming, water faucets turning on, and chairs rearranging themselves—all apparently without human interaction—are also commonly reported.

Some students have reported seeing shadowy figures, either near their beds or on a spiral staircase in one of the common areas. One student, whose books and papers regularly rearranged themselves, reported waking in the middle of the night to find a specter with red glowing eyes hovering over his bed. The figure pointed at him and then disappeared.

In recent years, the Blue Nun phenomenon has apparently spread beyond Gilmora Hall, with students reporting incidents in neighbouring Camden and Marguerite Halls. Despite these reports, however, residents don't seem put off by the idea of sharing their living quarters with a ghost, and most consider the potential for late night hauntings to be part of the character of life in Mount St. Bernard.

Reports of apparitions in the common rooms and lounges, belongings rearranged and tidied in unkempt rooms, and footsteps echoing down empty hallways are common. Students are warned when they move in that they should keep their chair tucked into their desk to prevent the Blue Nun from sitting and watching over them through the night.

The priest is less commonly spoken of, probably because his hauntings take place in the parts of the building that house offices and classrooms and are occupied only during the day. However, there have been rare claims in the past that the figure of a man watches as people climb the stairs.

Although many of the stories surrounding the Mount have died down in recent years, they still surface from time to time and whether you believe in ghosts or not, you have to admit that the stories of the Blue Nun are compelling, indeed.

Ghost Ships

What would a collection of ghost stories of Nova Scotia be without a story on haunted ships? Here are two of the province's most famous haunted ship stories.

The Northumberland Strait, a tidal water body between Prince Edward Island and the coast of eastern New Brunswick and northern Nova Scotia, extends 225 kilometres west-northwest to east-southeast from Cap-Lumière, New Brunswick, to Cape George, Nova Scotia. It is four to 17 kilometres in width and is 68 metres deep at its eastern end, but less than 20 metres deep over a large central area.

Geographically speaking, the Northumberland Strait is a natural wonder. Supernaturally speaking, it is a place of wonderment. The coastal communities that border the Northumberland Strait have long registered a variety of paranormal activity.

Stories of haunted houses, ghost ships and buried treasure, guarded by the spirits of bloodthirsty buccaneers, are mainstays of many local legends. One of the most popular and well-known stories is that of the burning ship of the strait.

The story goes back several centuries to when a large, two-masted ship caught fire out on the strait. It was a tragedy. People were burned or drowned when they tried to swim to shore.

The ghost ship of the Northumberland Strait really is the standard story of a ship on fire. However, for those who have seen it firsthand, it is very real. Over the years, many witnesses have insisted that they have actually seen the burning ship.

For instance, one woman who lived in an older home, built on a piece of property that abutted right onto the Northumberland Strait, says she saw the burning ship on Christmas Eve. It was very, very late, and as she happened to look out her kitchen window and across the strait, there it was, burning brightly out on the water.

Of course, it was in the middle of winter and there was ice in the strait. She knew this could not be any ordinary ship. This woman says she could see people jumping and screaming and could hear a great deal of noise. She also remembers that the fire was very bright—unnaturally bright. She knew that it was the ghost ship. What else could it be?

Then there is the story of two young men from the Pugwash area of Nova Scotia who saw the ship one night, and they were never the same again. Apparently, the two young men were coming off a night of revelry and were walking home along the shore, just having a good time, when they saw a burning ship out on the water. They were very concerned for the safety of the people on board because the fire looked really bad. It seems they had never heard the stories of the mysterious burning ship.

The two men hurried down the shore to a little dock that they knew was there. Once at the dock, they got into a small boat and started rowing toward the burning vessel. They rowed and rowed until they thought they should have reached the ship, but it was gone. It was nowhere to be seen. When they turned around to look back to shore, there it was, behind them. Somehow, the two young men had rowed right through the burning ship.

Needless to say, the men didn't take the same route back to shore.

But the haunted ship of the Northumberland Strait isn't the only ghost ship that is said to ply the waters around Nova Scotia.

St. Stephen's Anglican Church in Chester is said to have a unique connection to the legend of The Young Teazer.

Legend has it that a ghostly burning pirate ship named The Young Teazer haunts Mahone Bay. It is said that on summer nights when the moon is full, a flaming ghost of the ship Young Teazer can be seen moving across Mahone Bay.

In 1813, The Young Teazer was trapped by a British warship in Mahone Bay. The ship's captain Frederick

Johnson knew that the game was up. He and his crew faced either imprisonment or death by hanging. Rather than allowing their ship to be captured, the pirates threw a torch into the ship's powder magazine, causing a huge explosion. The ship was blown out of the water in a fiery blaze, killing the captain and most of the ship's crew.

The chase of The Young Teazer had come to an un-expectedly abrupt end, apparently at the hands of her own crew. Eight survivors out of the 36-member crew were plucked by the British from the waters near Naas Island on June 27, 1813.

A year after the explosion, locals began reporting sightings of a ship resembling The Young Teazer, burning on the horizon. Whenever rescue boats were sent out to investigate, the burning ship simply vanished into thin air.

Over the years, hundreds of people have seen a burning ship out on the Bay. Those who saw The Young Teazer up close, claimed there were men moving about on her decks, engulfed in flames and running back and forth in a panic. Others even reported hearing the tor-tured cries of the dead pirates who have been trying to escape their burning ship for more than a century.

But one small detail dealing with the final resting place of the little marauder has been lost in the develop-ment of the modern mythology surrounding The Young Teazer. While the chase itself did indeed take the vessel through the vast, sprawling waters of Mahone Bay, the fiery end of the adventure actually occurred some dis-tance from what would become the town of Mahone Bay, in the waters off Chester.

There is an interesting footnote to The Young Teazer legend. St. Stephen's Anglican Church, built in 1840, is located at the top of a knoll near the corner of Regent and Central Streets in Chester. In 1836, the parish determined that the congregation of St. Stephen's Church had outgrown the original building and four years later it was demolished. Within a week, the new church was sufficiently advanced in its construction, so regular service began there in June 1840. Tradition maintains that the small wooden cross that hangs in the church is made from a section of the keel of The Young Teazer.

Island Lore

With so many islands located off the coast of Nova Scotia, one would expect at least a few ghost stories or legends connected to these crops of land. For example, a few kilometres off the shore from Lunenburg, a small piece of land protrudes from the Atlantic Ocean and is known as Sacrifice Island.

According to legend, the Island was named when early settlers, mostly of German and French descent, moved into what is now known as Lunenburg County. Conflict quickly erupted between the settlers and the native people.

According to those same legends, one summer evening, a band of natives carried away several white children from a small settlement that had sprung up along the mainland somewhere in the area of what is now Mahone Bay. From the shore, it is said, the white children were taken to Sacrifice Island where they met their untimely demise. As time rolled on, the island became known as Sacrifice Island.

Since no documentation can be found to support this claim, the story is understood to be more folklore than fact. However, locals vehemently believe something tragic did happen there. Throughout the past two centuries, local seamen have reported seeing lights from Sacrifice Island.

As no one lives on the island, they concluded the lights must be the spirits of the children killed there.

The famous hand print of Payzant Island.

Here's another. On May 8, 1756, on a 108-acre island strategically stationed in what is today known as Mahone Bay, Louis Payzant was murdered and scalped, but not before leaving his mark on the landscape of local folk-lore. At the same time, a 12-year-old boy, a servant and her child also met their untimely fates on Covey Island, once known as Payzant Island.

The legend that surrounds the killings on the Island is best known locally for the bloody handprint that is embla-zoned on a rock that sits a fair distance from where it is believed the Payzant homestead was located more than 250 years ago.

Science suggests that the markings are the result of iron deposits that have rusted in the rock. However, the folklore story is much more fascinating. The story of the bloody handprint begins with the epic journey of

Marie Anne Payzant when, as a Huguenot, she fled from France to Jersey to escape religious persecution. In Jersey, Marie Anne met and married Louis Payzant, who had also fled to Jersey to escape Catholicism.

In 1753, the couple and their four children left a comfortable life on the island of Jersey and sailed across the Atlantic to settle in Lunenburg and, in 1755, built a home on Payzant Island, now Covey Island, in Mahone Bay. Within a year, a Maliseet raiding party, which was loyal to the French, landed on the Island, killed and scalped Louis and the three others previously mentioned, and took a pregnant Marie Anne and her children captive.

It is said that in the last few minutes of his life, Louis grabbed his bleeding chest, and in one last act of desperation, fell back onto a rock beside the front door, bracing himself with his bloody hand. The intense heat from the burning cabin seared the handprint into the boulder, where it can still be seen today. The rock has since been moved down the hill, where it sits near the beach.

As for Marie Anne and the Payzant children, the Maliseet raiders took the family to Quebec by canoe. Marie Anne was kept as a prisoner of war for four years, and the children were adopted by the Maliseet tribe and the Jesuits. Marie Anne and her children survived the ordeal and eventually made their way back to Nova Scotia. They settled in Falmouth, where Marie Anne remarried and lived to be 85.

This is the entrance to the famous Oak Island Money Pit. It is the spot where the legend began several hundred years ago.

A collection of Nova Scotia's legendary islands would be incomplete without the world-famous Oak Island, located just off the rugged, yet picturesque, coast near Western Shore, Lunenburg County. This mysterious place has attracted treasure seekers from around the world for centuries. The mystique and aura that surround Oak Island date back to 1795, when the hunt for an elusive treasure began.

Theories abound as to what is buried beneath the rocky, course soil of this small island that has spawned dozens of books and countless ghost stories. Many men have lost fortunes and their lives trying to solve the clues, hoping to ultimately unlock the treasure vault, but to date, the island has refused to give up its secret.

Perhaps the most popular of those theories is that it is a rich booty buried there by a band of bloodthirsty pirates, most notably Captain Kidd, who plied the waters of the Atlantic Ocean hundreds of years ago. Other theories suggest the stash is ancient Inca treasure or that it is the lost manuscripts of William Shakespeare. Some even theorize that the treasure is the Arc of the Covenant, hidden there by the Knights Templar, who were known to have visited the New World long before other early European explorers. The theories are as limited as one's imagination.

Legend has it that the mystery of Oak Island began in 1795, when a young Daniel McGinnis set out in the early morning hours to row to the island to investigate lights that had been reported there. Some locals said it was restless spirits while others whispered of pirates and buried treasure.

While on the island, McGinnis discovered a clearing in the midst of an oak tree stand. Someone had clearly cut down several trees. The boy also noticed that there was a visible depression in the centre of the clearing, about four metres in diameter, where the soil had obviously been disturbed, replaced and then allowed to settle. A block and tackle, attached to an oak branch hanging from a nearby tree over the centre of the depression, deepened the mystery.

McGinnis immediately became convinced that he had stumbled upon the location of a long forgotten deposit of pirate bounty. Hurrying back to shore, he convinced two friends to return to the island with him. Almost immediately, their efforts were rewarded. Two feet into the depression, they found a layer of intentionally placed flat stones. Digging further they saw that a shaft, about seven feet wide and walled with clay, had been sunk into the surface of Oak Island.

And so began the great Oak Island treasure hunt, but the truth is, whatever treasures are buried beneath the ground on the fabled Oak Island, remains just as much a mystery today, as it did over 200 years ago. Legend has it that seven must die before the truth treasure of Oak Island is found. Now that's a legend.

Local Legends: Sasquatch, Werewolves and UFOs

Photo by Vernon Oickle

The village of Shag Harbour on Nova Scotia's South Shore is the sight of one Canada's most famous UFO reports.

Does Sasquatch roam in Cape Breton?

So is Bigfoot—or Sasquatch as we call them in Canada—like the elusive cougar in Nova Scotia, in that people "believe" they exist, but can't exactly prove it?

The word "Sasquatch" comes from the native Salish language and means "wild man" or "hairy man." For the record, Sasquatch is a Canadian term. In the United States, the creature is known as Bigfoot.

Many people say that they know the Sasquatch exists in this part of the North American continent and some even insist they've seen them, but no one has seen one up close, nor has anyone ever produced any proof that such a creature exists anywhere in the province. However, that does not mean that people don't believe in the existence of these creatures. In fact, there have been several documented reports of people seeing "something" they couldn't explain.

Aboriginal and First Nations People have reported sightings and encounters with the Sasquatch that go back over hundreds of years. One of the earliest recorded sightings of a Sasquatch by a white man in Canada was reported in 1811, near what is today known as Jasper in Alberta, and was made by a fur trader and mapmaker named David Thompson. Closer to home, there have been reported sightings in the mountains of Cape Breton over the years.

One such sighting reportedly occurred in September 1997 while Matt, a young man from Cape Breton who insists on only his first name being used, was enjoying a late summer hike through the rolling foothills around South Mountain. He recalls the incident very well, he says, pointing out that while the morning started off cool, by early afternoon the temperatures had climbed in the mid- twenties. He is also sure that it was not fall yet as only a very few leaves had started to change colour, meaning the underbrush was still quite thick, which he points out, accounts for his difficulty in actually seeing whatever it was that was following him that day.

"I like to hike alone because I like the solitude in that it gives me time to think," Matt begins. "I don't bring any kind of electronic listening device with me because I prefer to hear the sounds of nature and I don't like having anyone else with me because I don't like to hear other people talking when I'm hiking. I just like to be one with nature and I don't believe you can have a complete experience if you have other distractions around you."

He says that whenever he goes for a hike, he carries a cellphone with him just in case of an emergency. He stresses though that he doesn't take calls and or listen to music when he's hiking.

On this particular day, Matt recalls that he had been walking for about an hour, when he suddenly began feeling as though he weren't alone, and occasionally he could hear sounds of someone—or something—walking through the woods and underbrush.

"I was sticking to a designated trail," he explains, "so at first I just thought that maybe it was another hiker out enjoying a later summer stroll through the woods, but as I looked around and scoped out the trail in front and behind me, I couldn't see anyone."

"At first," Matt says, "I just shrugged it off because I know that sometimes when you're deep in the woods, even the smallest noise can sound major. And, you can get jumpy when you're out there because you're always thinking what if it were some sort of wild animal like a bear or coyote? But I didn't see anything like that."

As he pushed on, Matt says he continued to hear the sounds of movement all around him, but no matter how often he stopped to scan his surroundings, he could not locate the origins of the noise.

"I thought maybe it was birds or a porcupine but then I realized that no matter where I went or how quickly I moved along the trail, whatever was following me was keeping up the same pace," Matt recalls. "If it were a bird or animal, it wouldn't do that—unless it was stalking me."

"At one point," Matt says, "the sounds coming from the bushes got just a little too close for comfort. I couldn't see anything, but there was one spot on the trail where I had this strange sensation that whatever was out there, had come so close to me that it probably could have touched me, but the bushes were so thick and dense that I couldn't see far beyond the trail and honestly, there was no way I was leaving the trail to investigate," he says. "I called out a couple of times to see if anyone was there, but I didn't get an answer. It really freaked me out."

Matt has hiked many different places across Canada and has been doing so for many years, but he points out, he has never before or since that day, felt anything like what he experienced in that region of Cape Breton.

"I'm not saying it was Bigfoot," he says. "I am not even suggesting that, but I am telling you that whatever it was that followed me that day, it wasn't animal either. I've hiked around animals many times in the past and I have never experienced anything like that before. It wasn't an animal and if there were someone else out there, then they did a pretty damned good job of scaring me because I don't scare easily."

Matt isn't alone. In fact, there have been other reported sightings of Sasquatch in Cape Breton. This report from March 26, 2103, was found on a web site devoted to Sasquatch-Bigfoot sightings around North America.

"I am an avid amateur photographer and have always loved hiking and exploring. Nature has always fascinated me. Even as young children, my brother and I would camp for days with almost no food or supplies to test ourselves in a remote wooded area. I remember clearly finding what I can only describe as a nest large enough for us both to climb inside and the eerie feelings that got us out of there," the report reads.

"We lived on Cape Breton Island and although, while growing up, I only ever heard stories from my mother and one other story long after I had moved to Alberta,

I did once see what I believe to be a Sasquatch. I was 12 years old and did not see its face but I did see it walking through alders. Although it was twilight, I did get a clear view. It was walking and moving the brush with its hands and grabbing as it walked slightly hunched. I was frozen in a squatted position for at least a minute until it was far away enough for me to not be seen. I still have a clear memory of that evening and have been fascinated ever since."

Another report reads, "When I was between seven and nine years old, five or six other kids and I were playing in a stream on the South Mountain of Nova Scotia. On weekends, most of the family would get together at my grandmother's so all the kids would always hang out at a pond that was shaped like a bathtub and you could lay in there and a small waterfall would run down over your neck. After running up and down the mountain, it was nice to get in and cool off. One afternoon near suppertime we were just doing our usual splashing each other and stuff. It was getting late when something started throwing rocks all around us, but nobody was hit by even one rock. Good thing, because when I look back they were some big rocks."

The poster continues, "When we started to run up the animal trail that led to my grandmother's place, whatever had thrown the rocks made a very fast exit. We got to my grandmother's to see if it was just family messing with us, but they were all there playing cards and didn't know what the hell we were talking about. I don't know what threw the rocks, but by the size of them it wasn't your average person, and the speed it got up over the brook bank, I mean scared kids move pretty damn fast and this thing was gone."

"I don't recall any smell or anything like that and we weren't looking for any tracks. I had never even thought about Bigfoot at that time in my life. It was only years later when we were all in our teens sitting around at one of the other kids place that the possibility of it being a Sasquatch came up. I don't know what it was but, whatever it was, it didn't try to hurt us, but it didn't want us there on that day. I will never forget that."

While these accounts offer no scientific proof or physical proof that Sasquatch roams the mountains of Cape Breton, it is clear that something left an impact on this trio of possible witnesses.

Are there werewolves in Lunenburg?

Now a UNESCO World Heritage site, the seaside port of Lunenburg has had more than its fair share of strange and macabre stories passed down over the years, beginning with its early days as a British settlement.

German, Swiss and French foreign Protestants who arrived at the South Shore port in 1753 to establish an English presence in an area once dominated by the Mi'kmaq and French, brought their own brand of superstitions with them, beliefs that often resulted in the creation of some very interesting, and often frightening, tales. One such account involves a man who came to be known as the Lunenburg Wehr Wulf.

While the origins of this story are not clear, a detailed chronicle of the events that earned him a place in the darker side of the town's past, was written by author Theodore Hennigar and published in the local paper, the Lunenburg Progress Enterprise on April 12, 1963. The tale begins in December 1755, when a French girl named Nanette managed to escape to the woods after British troops had invaded and destroyed the village where she lived in the Cornwallis Valley, now the Annapolis Valley.

After a period of wandering in the wilderness, she came upon a Mi'kmaq settlement where she was taken in, cared for and treated as one of their own. Days later, Nanette appeared with a female Mi'kmaq elder at a small German settlement on the outskirts of present-day Lunenburg where they encountered an old woman who took an immediate liking to the young girl, expressing a desire to adopt her.

An agreement was struck and, after Nanette was traded for a crimson handkerchief, she again was back in a white family where she grew into a charming young woman with a beautiful face, manners, amiable disposition and a magnetic power of making friends among both young and old.

While those qualities attracted a variety of suitors, Nanette's affections fell to one Hans Gerhardt, "a finely built German lad of the community who had a particular temper."

The two married, and for a time enjoyed an idyllic marriage in which they were extremely devoted to each other.

Soon they were blessed with a baby daughter, an event which, rather than enhancing their affections for each other, had a strangely opposite effect.

"It seemed Hans was incapable of understanding the love of Nanette for her daughter," Mr. Hennigar wrote. "He became jealous and moody, falling into violent fits of temper over nothing, feeding his peculiar mind with fuel for the fires of self-pity which raged within."

Occupied with her newborn child, Nanette did not realize for some time that something was amiss with her husband. When she finally did, she took it for granted that he had become ill, perhaps from working too hard on their farm. Hans then began to display even more erratic behaviour, and began sleeping in the kitchen, apart from his wife, saying the baby was disturbing him as he tried to rest.

He also took to wandering from their home at night, a practice that became more and more regular and one which he would not discuss with his wife when she questioned him of his activities. It was at that time that strange tales of a mysterious nightly presence, manlike, but able to run swiftly on all fours, began circulating in the community. Farmers started finding their lambs lying dead in the morning with their throats torn from ear to ear, and the blood gone from their bodies.

At first, bears were suspected as the culprit, but it was reasoned that that could not be the case, since the meat of the animals was not taken, nor was it consumed. Hans joined the hunters who were trying to find whatever beast was killing the lambs, but no culprit could be uncovered.

That summer, with the blueberries in full ripeness, Hans left the family home one afternoon with a basket to harvest the fruit. After rocking the baby asleep, Nanette left the child at home and joined her husband in the fields. His basket full, he returned to the house to empty it.

Soon realizing that her husband had been gone a long time, and thinking that something might have happened to the baby, Nanette raced home where she discovered that both daughter and husband were missing. A search party was hastily arranged, and those men entered the woods where they came upon a gurgling brook, and Hans Gerhardt crouching low over the water.

"At their approach, he sprang up with a snarling cry and turned upon them with animal fury," Mr. Hennigar wrote. "The strong men soon subdued him, however, and tied him up. There were bloodstains on his arms, and a wet spot on his blue linen blouse. 'Mon Dieu! He has killed her,' Nanette shrieked. Hans tried to spring at her, but the men had done a good job of tying him and his struggle was in vain."

Hans was taken to Lunenburg, jailed, and sentenced to die for his alleged crime, but that eventuality never took place. When his cell was opened the next morning, he lay dead on the floor, the veins of his arms ripped open by his own teeth, which caused him to bleed to death.

He was buried in a nameless grave on Gallows Hill and the legend of the Lunenburg Wehr Wulf was born. Or was it?

A check of burial records with staff at the Hillcrest Cemetery, which includes all recorded burials including those in the "poor lots" section of Gallows Hill, shows no burial of a Hans Gerhardt. A similar investigation of the names of foreign Protestants who resettled Lunenburg in 1753 reveals one Johannes Gerhardt, but that individual, who was born in Germany in 1724, was married to an Anna Griesterland and did not die until 1795.

Local historian Stephen Ernst says that Mr. Hennigar's publication in the Progress Enterprise in 1963 is the oldest written account of the tale that he is aware of, and it was written very much like a story.

"So I really don't know how much of this is actually true," he says. "But if it was conjured up, it's been around for the last 50 years, at least, and who knows how much longer."

Is There Life Out There?

That depends upon who you ask, but if you were in the tiny village of Shag Harbour on Nova Scotia's South

Shore on the night of October 4, 1967, you might be inclined to answer in the affirmative.

Shortly after 11 p.m., witnesses reported that a UFO, estimated at 60 feet in diameter, was seen hovering over the water. Those who saw the object reported that they saw four bright lights that flashed in a uniform pattern. After hovering for several minutes, witnesses said the object tilted and quickly descended toward the water. Witnesses, who immediately called the nearby RCMP detachment located in Barrington Passage, reported a bright flash and an explosion. The immediate thought was that an aircraft had plunged into the icy Atlantic. The rush was on as there could be survivors.

With the calls coming in, three RCMP officers were dispatched to the scene, two approaching from east of the site, while a third who was on highway patrol on Highway 3, headed to the impact site from the West. When the three officers met they found that the object was still floating on the water about a half-mile from shore. It was glowing a pale yellow and was leaving a trail of dense yellow foam as it drifted in the ebb tide. Witnesses later reported that the object had changed shape several times before hitting the water.

Neither the rescue co-ordination centre in Halifax, nor the nearby NORAD radar facility at Baccaro, had any knowledge of missing aircraft, either civilian or military. Also, a coast guard lifeboat dispatched from nearby Clark's Harbour, along with several local fishing boats were sent to the crash site, but the UFO had submerged before they reached the location. However, the sulphurous-smelling yellow foam continued to bubble to the surface from the point where the UFO went down. In a matter of time, a 120 by 300 foot slick developed. Search efforts continued until 3 a.m., and then resumed

166

at first light the next day, as it was clear that something had gone into the water.

The next morning, a preliminary report was sent to Canadian Forces Headquarters in Ottawa. After communicating with NORAD, Maritime Command was asked to conduct an underwater search as soon as possible for the object. Seven navy divers from the HMCS Granby searched for several days throughout the daylight hours until October 8. On October 9, Maritime Command cancelled the search saying nothing was found.

In time, the Shag Harbour UFO became Case #34 in the infamous Condon Committee Report, but whatever the object was remains a mystery even today. This incident is the only UFO crash recorded and recognized by the Canadian Government.

So there you have it. Proof positive that Sasquatch, werewolves and UFOs do exist in Nova Scotia.